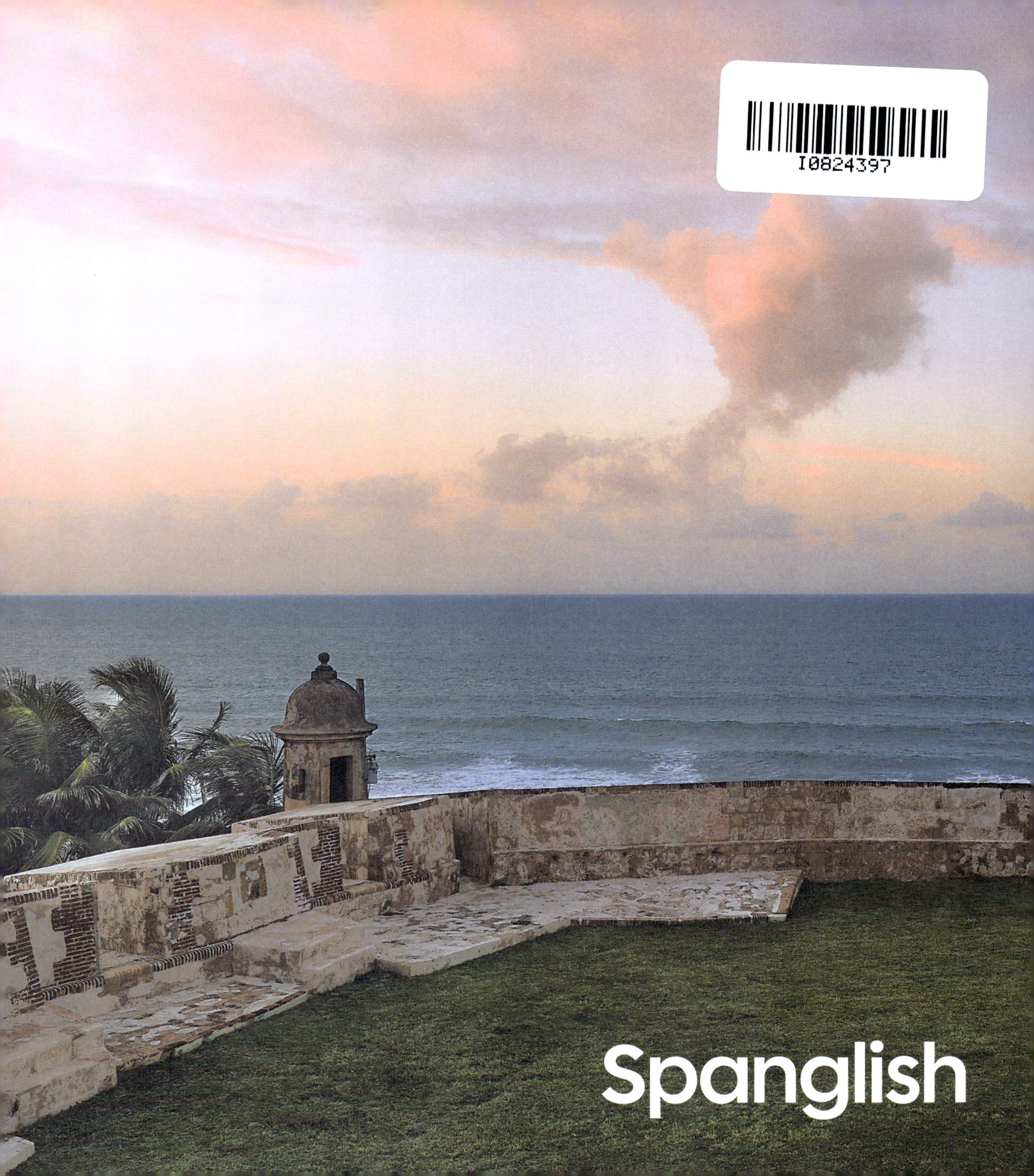

Spanglish

Spanglish

Recipes & Stories

Monti Carlo

SIMON ELEMENT

New York Amsterdam/Antwerp London Toronto
Sydney/Melbourne New Delhi

An Imprint of Simon & Schuster, LLC
1230 Avenue of the Americas
New York, NY 10020

Photographer: Rafael N. Ruiz Mederos
Food Stylist: Keila Rivera
Recipe Tester: Bonnie Benwick

First Simon Element hardcover edition May 2026

Manufactured in China

1 3 5 7 9 10 8 6 4 2

Library of Congress Control Number has been applied for.

ISBN 978-1-6680-2218-4

ISBN 978-1-6680-2219-1 (ebook)

For Puerto Rico, *mi patria* (my homeland), my first love, my inspiration.

For the chefs, friends, and family who've helped me find my voice.

And for me. Because at one point, I didn't think I could. *Mira pa ya.* (Look at that.)

Part Three

A Puerto Rican Learns to Speak Spanglish 154

Foreword

Make no mistake—when a chef named Monti Carlo first walked through the doors to compete on the hit series *MasterChef*, I had no idea what kind of chef I'd get. It was better than I could have hoped for: I found a high-energy, no-BS single mom who was willing to give everything she had to be crowned America's next MasterChef.

It was Season 3 of the series, and her flair and passion weren't just present when the stage lights were on–they were in every dish that hit the judges' podium. She was ferocious and made it all the way to the Top 5, which was an incredible achievement. She faced some extremely tough competition along her journey on the show, but her passion–and her drive to make her family proud–kept her fueled throughout the competition. Needless to say, I truly believed that when the doors to the *MasterChef* kitchen closed, the doors to her culinary journey had only just opened.

Since watching her leaving *MasterChef,* I've always kept a close eye on Monti, even after she was off the airwaves. She put her head down, focused on learning, and honed her skills—all while staying true to herself. From Food Network to even my YouTube channel, I've seen Monti grow into the remarkable cook she is today, embracing the food she grew up eating and sharing it with her family.

That's why I'm so proud of this book. It's a culmination of Monti's passion for food, family, and her heritage. Although Monti only spent a part of her childhood in Puerto Rico, many of the recipes in this book transport me back to the incredible island I fell in love with years ago while filming my National Geographic show *Uncharted.* But her food is also filled with continental twists. From her drinks and spice mixes to her breakfasts, condiments, main courses, and incredible desserts, every recipe in this book is a marriage of flavors, of cultures, and of taste.

I've already made a few of the recipes, but I can't wait to cook everything in this book for my family so they can experience the unique Spanglish flavors firsthand.

But this book isn't just recipes—it's very much Monti's DNA. Through the stories, personal anecdotes, and memories Monti has woven throughout, you gain a deep understanding of how and why Monti has grown so much in her culinary career.

So whether you're cooking for your family, your friends, or your Abuela, you'll find that Monti has given you everything you need in this book. I can't wait for everyone to see what I've always seen: Monti's incredible culinary talent.

Enjoy,
Gordon

Introduction

Is it possible to be two people at once?

It's 1982, and Héctor Lavoe's "Mi Gente" erupts in waves of increasing magnitude from my mother's giant walnut-grained Pioneer speakers. I eye the stereo's silver volume knob. It sits as big as a coffee cup behind a glass door that still reeks of Windex.

It's Saturday morning, our family's weekly Puerto Rican music-packed cleaning extravaganza. But we're not living in San Juan anymore; we're living in Houston. I'm seven years old, and it's time for the great *yanqui* (yankee) tradition of Saturday morning cartoons. Except, I can barely hear what Scooby Doo is up to as Héctor chants, *"La! La! La! La! La! La! La!"*

I glance quickly at my mother, who is now belting Spanish lyrics at the popcorn ceiling of our two-bedroom apartment as her feet move furiously, tapping, side stepping, stomping, and kicking. One hand holds the broom handle as a microphone stand. The other is raised and moves like an exclamation point after every word. *"¡Que! ¡Cante! ¡Mi! ¡Gente!"* ("Let my people sing!")

She dances up to me and points to the TV, *"Mira, apaga eso* (turn that off) and clean me the table." She pivots to the stereo, opens the glass door, and turns the music up even louder. There will be no more English-language cartoons today. The trumpets of Héctor's orchestra have triumphed. I twist the TV's power switch to the left, grab a *pañito* (rag), and start dusting our coffee table.

That cacophony between English and Spanish has been the soundtrack of my life, a constant tug-of-war between two languages, two cultures, two versions of myself that never quite fit into either world.

Being bicultural is a difficult concept to understand unless you've experienced it. But I'm assuming that if you have this book in your hands, you know a little something about it. When you're a Puerto Rican living in the continental US, it means learning to code-switch faster than Gordon Ramsay chops an onion.

You must remember to shake hands with the people who prefer to speak English, and go in for a hug and a kiss with those who prefer to speak Spanish. You learn to regulate the volume of your voice at your school friend's house and how not to get lost in the loud, vibrant chaos of a Latino family gathering. Your life becomes a collision of Spanish and English.

Growing up, I felt like I was perpetually bridging the gap between worlds, never fully belonging to either. In the eyes of my Houston classmates, my mother's brightly patterned hand-me-downs were something I should not be proud to wear. The leftovers in my lunchbox did not match their miniature bags of potato chips, juice boxes, and pale sandwiches made with processed cheese and bologna. Instead, last night's *sancocho* (stew) sat in an air-tight container that could contain everything except the smell of the savory stew. The thick broth stained every bit of its plastic vessel a dull yellow, like leaving a mark was some sort of Olympic sport. It branded me as well, of course. It tied me to a population that understood what that faded yellow blotch meant. Though that population wasn't always welcoming either.

Among my island peers, I was the "Americanized" one. My English was flawless, but my Spanish, my native tongue, was broken. If someone talked to me in Spanish, I answered them in English and ignored the judgment in their eyes. I could not dance to salsa or merengue, while my cousins on the island could move their feet in the confusing sequence with their eyes closed. And then there were my blank stares at Puerto Rican pop culture references that they thought I'd understand if they repeated them louder, as if volume could bridge the gap.

Most of my life felt like performance–shape-shifting, shrinking, and stretching to fit what was expected of me. I spent years trying to be enough for both sides, hiding one part of myself to be accepted by the other. It wasn't until everything fell apart in my late thirties, after my marriage disintegrated, my career came to a screeching halt, and my savings ran out, that I found refuge in Spanglish. It's a secret language understood only by Latinos who straddle borders, who navigate the hyphen between two irreconcilable ways of living. They are done being what other people want them to be. They don't need to be filed away neatly. They just want to be. It is a collective *"¡Déjame en paz!"* ("Leave me in peace!")

Spanglish is a rebellion against the expectation of choosing sides. It's a mosaic of borrowed words and mangled grammar, a testament to the bittersweet beauty of fusing two very different ways of life. It's the language of belonging, not to either or, but to the tangled, vibrant space in between. A space where I can lose myself in the intersection between worlds. A space where I can fully fit in.

This cookbook is more than just recipes. It's a reflection on identity, a love letter to my heritage, and a testament to the healing power of food.

Within these pages, you'll find tales of my childhood on the island, the challenges of migrating to the big continent, and the moments of joy and confusion that come with growing up bicultural. You'll also discover the dishes embodying that journey: continental American classics created with the bold flavors of Puerto Rico, a taste of both worlds coming together in perfect harmony. I make my Texas elementary school's soupy chili with my Abuela Dora's sweet and savory picadillo, cinnamon rolls constructed with pillowy *mallorca* (sweet bun) dough, and *bacalaíto* battered onion rings.

If you're not familiar with Puerto Rican cuisine, it was born from colonization. It's the result of the collision of Taíno indigenous ingredients, Spanish colonial staples, and African culinary traditions brought by enslaved people. Many of my little island's signature dishes were first created from the meager scraps enslaved women were given to feed their loved ones. Their hands might have been shackled, but the magic embedded in their fingertips could not be restrained.

That's why Puerto Rican recipes like sancocho can boast a seemingly long list of ingredients. Each addition wasn't just about flavor but about using every available resource, a dozen odds and ends combined to make one delicious whole. It's a philosophy that applies not just to cooking but to life itself—a reminder that even from fragments, we can create something beautiful and nourishing.

That said, most of the recipes are easy to make. For the more complicated dishes, I've noted what you can do to save a little hassle. For my vegetarian and vegan friends, I've provided substitutions to make dishes plant-forward. And since there are more Puerto Ricans in the continental US than on the island, I've included substitutions for traditional ingredients that can be hard to come by at neighborhood supermarkets.

Making something from nothing is a thread woven throughout my life and throughout these recipes. It is a reminder of the resilience of Puerto Rican culture and the strength that comes from embracing all parts of ourselves. It's a legacy I'm honored to carry on in my kitchen and one I invite you to explore alongside me.

I hope these recipes do for you what they do for me: remind you that home isn't just a place but a feeling you can create anywhere, one delicious bite at a time. *Bienvenidos y buen provecho*. (Welcome and enjoy.)

Ingredient Glossary

The sight of Puerto Rican ingredients instantly transports me back to my Abuela Dora's kitchen. The small fold out card table we ate most of our meals on was rusty at the hinges but covered in a joyful blue vinyl cloth splashed with a red tropical flower print. A lone bottle of *pique* (hot sauce) loomed like a giant over a white plastic salt shaker that held down a stack of dimpled paper napkins. There were various bowls on the lone counter, some with green plantains and avocados from our trees, others with bitter oranges and guavas. The earthy aroma of *recao* (culantro) steaming over rice in a caldero infused every square inch of that small room.

Recreating those vibes can be daunting in the Lower 48. Searching for traditional island ingredients at chain grocery stores can leave you frustrated and empty-handed, especially in the Latino or "ethnic" foods aisle, where a sense of "otherness" becomes a physical place. Dozens of cultures are compounded into a monolith and reduced to a few inches of shelf space. It's a constant reminder that it doesn't matter that we make up 20 percent of the population, we still don't belong. Our food is "exotic," a novelty, something to be explored, but never fully embraced.

You'll have better luck at neighborhood Latino or Asian markets. Of course, in today's connected world, your search for ingredients can extend far beyond supermarket aisles. Some of my favorite online grocery stores include:

antojoboricuapr.com
boricuaproduce.com
tienda.com (for sausages)
elcolmado.com (for candy and coffee)
saborapais.com (for pantry staples)

There are traditional Puerto Rican ingredients I use to create the dishes in this book. They might not be easy to come by, but they are definitely worth it! In the case that you can't find them, I have included substitutions.

Achiote

WHAT IS IT? A brick-red paste or powder made from annatto seeds.

TASTE: Earthy, slightly nutty, with peppery notes and a subtle sweetness.

USAGE: Mix into Sazón (page 33), add to meats, mashed roots, rice, stews, and sauces for color and flavor.

SUBSTITUTIONS: Blend paprika and turmeric in a 2:1 ratio.

Adobo

WHAT IS IT? A seasoning blend that typically contains salt, garlic powder, onion powder, oregano, white pepper, and sometimes cumin, coriander, and turmeric.

TASTE: Varies depending on the brand, but generally savory, salty, and garlicky.

USAGE: Season meats, vegetables, beans, and stews for a quick flavor boost.

SUBSTITUTIONS: Adobo (page 30)

Ají Peppers

WHAT IS IT? Small, sweet to moderately spicy peppers used extensively in Puerto Rican cuisine. Varieties range in heat level and color.

TASTE: Depending on the variety, from sweet and fruity to mildly hot with a bright, fresh pepper flavor.

USAGE: Used in Sofrito (page 38), Pique (page 41), sauces, stews, marinades, and can be pickled. Essential for flavoring many traditional dishes.

SUBSTITUTIONS: For a milder flavor, use sweet peppers, Cubanelle peppers, or red bell peppers. For a spicier option, use habañero or Scotch bonnet peppers, adjusting the quantity to taste.

Alcaparrado

WHAT IS IT? A mix of stuffed green olives and capers.

TASTE: Salty, sour, with a briny olive flavor and a sharp caper bite.

USAGE: Add to stews, sauces, and picadillo for a complex flavor profile.

SUBSTITUTIONS: Chopped green olives and capers.

Annatto Seeds

WHAT IS IT? Dried seeds from the achiote tree, often used for their vibrant red-orange color and mild earthy flavor. Common in Latin American, Caribbean, and Filipino cuisines.

TASTE: Mild, slightly peppery with a hint of nuttiness and earthiness.

USAGE: Infuse in oil to create Annatto Oil (page 37) for coloring and flavoring rice, meats, and stews, or grind and use as a spice rub.

SUBSTITUTIONS: a 2:1 mix of paprika and turmeric for color and a hint of flavor.

Bacalaíto Mix

WHAT IS IT? A mixture of flour, seasonings, and dried, salted codfish used to create a batter for fritters (*bacalaítos*).

TASTE: Salty, fishy, with a bit of sweetness.

USAGE: Rehydrate and mix into a batter for fritters.

SUBSTITUTIONS: See Bacalaítos (page 126) for a homemade mix

Naranja Agria (Bitter Orange)

WHAT IS IT? A citrus fruit similar to a Seville orange, used for marinades and sauces.

TASTE: Sour, bitter, and slightly floral.

USAGE: The juice is used in marinades for meats, particularly *lechón* (roasted pork).

SUBSTITUTIONS: A mix of lime, grapefruit, and orange juices in a 1:1:1 ratio.

Butifarra

WHAT IS IT? A white, simply seasoned pork sausage

TASTE: Savory, garlicky, with a hint of sweetness.

USAGE: Grilled, fried, used in soups and stews.

SUBSTITUTIONS: Mildly-flavored pork sausage.

Café

WHAT IS IT? Puerto Rican coffee is a dark robust roast.

TASTE: Strong, bold, and slightly sweet, with notes of chocolate and caramel.

USAGE: Brewed and enjoyed for breakfast, throughout the day, and as *cafecito* (espresso).

SUBSTITUTIONS: Strong espresso blend, dark roast coffee.

Calabaza

WHAT IS IT? A Caribbean pumpkin smaller than a traditional pumpkin, with a vibrant green skin and orange flesh.

TASTE: Sweet, slightly nutty, with a creamy texture.

USAGE: Used in soups, stews, roasts, and purees.

SUBSTITUTIONS: Butternut squash, acorn squash, kabocha squash, sweet potato.

Coconut

WHAT IS IT? The versatile fruit's flesh can be shredded, grated, or flaked. It can be sweetened or unsweetened.

TASTE: Sweet, creamy, with a tropical aroma.

USAGE: Shredded, grated, or flaked coconut adds texture to batters, baked goods, and sweets.

SUBSTITUTIONS: Finely chopped macadamia nuts.

Coconut Cream

WHAT IS IT? Coconut cream is coconut milk with less water and a higher fat content. It is thicker, like heavy cream.

TASTE: Subtly sweet with creamy, nutty undertones.

USAGE: Though often used in desserts, it's wonderful as a coconut milk substitute and creates thick, velvety sauces.

SUBSTITUTIONS: Coconut milk, Greek yogurt, heavy cream, vegan cream.

Coconut Milk

WHAT IS IT? A fatty white liquid created from coconut flesh with the consistency of cow's milk.

TASTE: Subtly sweet with creamy, nutty undertones.

USAGE: It adds richness and depth to both savory and sweet preparations and is used in everything from stews to desserts.

SUBSTITUTIONS: Almond milk or evaporated milk.

Cotija

WHAT IS IT? A crumbly Mexican cheese similar to feta cheese.

TASTE: Salty, tangy, slightly sour.

USAGE: Crumbled on salads and tacos.

SUBSTITUTIONS: Feta cheese, queso fresco, crumbled paneer.

Cream of Coconut

WHAT IS IT? A thick coconut cream blended with lots of sugar.

TASTE: Cloyingly sweet, creamy, rich, with a strong coconut taste.

USAGE: Used in desserts and tropical drink preparations.

SUBSTITUTIONS: Condensed milk made from coconut milk or whole milk.

Dulce de Papaya

WHAT IS IT? A thick preserve made from strips or chunks of papaya.

TASTE: Very sweet with a subtle papaya flavor.

USAGE: Often paired with farmer's cheese. It can be used as a topping for toast, pancakes, and ice cream, or as a filling for cakes and pastries.

SUBSTITUTIONS: Mango jam, apricot preserves.

Dulce de Leche

WHAT IS IT? A rich, caramelized milk spread.

TASTE: Sweet and creamy, with a hint of caramel and burnt sugar.

USAGE: Spread on pastries, mixed into cake batters, or used as a topping for ice cream.

SUBSTITUTIONS: Caramel spread.

Empanadilla Discs

WHAT IS IT? Premade dough circles used for making empanadillas.

TASTE: Neutral, slightly doughy.

USAGE: Filled with meat, seafood, vegetables, or cheese, then fried or baked.

SUBSTITUTIONS: wonton wrappers (for smaller empanadillas), pie dough (for a thicker, flakier crust).

Gandules (Pigeon Peas)

WHAT IS IT? Small, round legumes commonly used in Caribbean and Latin American cooking, especially in Puerto Rican dishes like Arroz con Gandules.

TASTE: Nutty, slightly sweet, and earthy with a firm bite.

USAGE: Simmered in rice dishes, stews, and soups. Often paired with Sofrito (page 38) and pork for added depth.

SUBSTITUTIONS: Black-eyed peas, green lentils.

Green Plantain

WHAT IS IT? Unripe banana-shaped fruit used in savory dishes like mofongo and tostones.

TASTE: Slightly sweet, starchy, and earthy when cooked.

USAGE: Boiled, mashed (mofongo), fried (tostones), or used in stews and soups.

SUBSTITUTIONS: Taro root (for mofongo), breadfruit (for tostones).

Guanabana (Soursop)

WHAT IS IT? A large, egg-shaped, spiky green fruit.

TASTE: Sweet, tangy, with a citrusy undertone.

USAGE: Used in juices, smoothies, ice cream, and desserts.

SUBSTITUTIONS: Pineapple or a combination of lime and star fruit.

Guava Paste

WHAT IS IT? A thick paste made from guava fruit.

TASTE: Sweet, tart, with a concentrated guava flavor.

USAGE: Layered into pastries and cakes, used in glazes, fillings, and sauces.

SUBSTITUTIONS: Guava jam, fig jam, apricot jam (with added lemon juice).

Guava Shells, frozen

WHAT IS IT? Guava fruit that are frozen whole. These are not a paste or packed in syrup.

TASTE: They have a sweet-tart flavor and soft texture.

USAGE: Use them as a topping or filling in desserts, or go savory and use them in sauces.

SUBSTITUTIONS: Fresh guava.

Hibiscus

WHAT IS IT? The dried flowers of the hibiscus plant are used to make a vibrant red tea (té de flor de Jamaica).

TASTE: Tart, tangy, with a slightly cranberry-like flavor.

USAGE: Steeped for hot or iced tea, used in cocktails, and as a flavoring in desserts.

SUBSTITUTIONS: Cranberry juice, pomegranate juice, tart cherry juice.

Longaniza

WHAT IS IT? This firm, coarse pork sausage is traditionally seasoned with annatto seeds (achiote), giving it its characteristic brick-red color. Though it's typically sold fresh, it can also be cured or smoked.

TASTE: Savory and garlicky, with a hint of sweetness from the annatto seeds.

USAGE: The sausage can be mixed into rice dishes, braised in soups and stews, or used as a stuffing for empanadilla and mofongo.

SUBSTITUTIONS: Spanish chorizo or mildly flavored Italian sausage.

Malta

WHAT IS IT? A nonalcoholic malt beverage.

TASTE: Sweet, malty, caramel-like.

USAGE: Enjoyed cold on its own, used in milkshakes and cocktails.

SUBSTITUTIONS: Root beer.

Mamey

WHAT IS IT? A large, egg-shaped light brown fruit with orange flesh.

TASTE: Sweet and creamy, with a subtle apricot and caramel flavor.

USAGE: Eaten fresh, used in milkshakes, smoothies, and ice cream.

SUBSTITUTIONS: Papaya, mango.

Masarepa

WHAT IS IT? Masarepa is a precooked corn flour with a fine texture.

TASTE: Masarepa has a mild corn flavor, similar but softer than a corn tortilla. Popular brands include P.A.N., Goya Masarepa, Bob's Red Mill, or Masa Harina.

USAGE: Masarepa is primarily used to make arepas, which are corn cakes, but it can also be used to create a variety of dishes like empanadillas, tamales, and even polenta.

SUBSTITUTIONS: Cornmeal can be used as a similar base for some recipes, although the texture and flavor will differ.

Morcilla

WHAT IS IT? A blood sausage similar to Spanish morcilla but often made with rice.

TASTE: Savory, garlicky, slightly sweet, earthy, and mild ironlike flavor.

USAGE: Grilled, fried.

SUBSTITUTIONS: Spanish morcilla, Korean blood sausage.

Passion Fruit

WHAT IS IT? A small, round purple fruit with yellow pulp.

TASTE: Tart, tangy, with tropical sweetness and texture from its black seeds.

USAGE: Drinks, sauces, desserts, and cocktails.

SUBSTITUTIONS: Lime juice with added sugar or orange and pineapple juice blend.

Pique

WHAT IS IT? A vinegar-based hot sauce made with *ají caballero* peppers and other chile peppers, garlic, spices, and sometimes fruit rinds like pineapple.

TASTE: Fiery, fruity, with a lingering vinegary heat.

USAGE: Added to taste for heat in various dishes, from stews to sauces.

SUBSTITUTIONS: Other vinegar-based hot sauces.

Queso Fresco

WHAT IS IT? A fresh, crumbly cheese.

TASTE: Mild, slightly salty, creamy.

USAGE: Crumbled on salads and tacos, used in dips and fillings. In Puerto Rico, it is often sliced and paired with guava paste.

SUBSTITUTIONS: Queso blanco, strained ricotta.

Recao

WHAT IS IT? A herb similar in flavor to cilantro but more pungent. Also known as culantro, Mexican coriander, Puerto Rican coriander, sawtooth coriander, and ngò gai.

TASTE: Herbaceous, grassy, citrusy, peppery.

USAGE: Used fresh in Recaíto (page 34), sauces, and marinades.

SUBSTITUTIONS: Cilantro leaves combined with cilantro stems will recreate recao's robust flavor.

Recaíto

WHAT IS IT? A green puree or finely chopped salsa made with recao (culantro), onions, garlic, peppers, and spices.

TASTE: Herbaceous, garlicky, peppery, with a hint of sweetness from ají peppers.

USAGE: Used as a flavor base in stews, soups, marinades, and sauces.

SUBSTITUTIONS: Recaíto (page 34)

Rice, Medium-Grain

WHAT IS IT? Medium-grain white rice is the staple starch in Puerto Rican cuisine.

TASTE: Neutral, starchy, absorbs the flavors of other ingredients.

USAGE: Served alongside main dishes, used in desserts.

SUBSTITUTIONS: long-grain white rice or short-grain white rice with adjustments of the liquid to rice ratio.

Puerto Rican Rum

WHAT IS IT? A light and smooth distilled alcoholic spirit made primarily from sugarcane byproducts (like molasses) and produced in Puerto Rico.

TASTE: Varies depending on type and age, but often has vanilla, caramel, molasses, and tropical fruit notes. It can range from crisp and slightly sweet (in white rums) to rich, warm, and oaky (in aged or dark rums).

USAGE: Used in cocktails like piña colada and mojito, in dessert sauces, and to add depth to stews and marinades.

SUBSTITUTIONS: Brandy, cachaça, whiskey.

Sazón

WHAT IS IT? An orange-hued seasoning blend typically containing salt, garlic powder, onion powder, oregano, cumin, achiote, and other spices.

TASTE: Savory, warm, with a touch of smokiness from the achiote.

USAGE: Season meats, vegetables, beans, and rice for a quick flavor boost and to add a golden hue.

SUBSTITUTIONS: Sazón (page 33) or Adobo (page 30).

Sofrito

WHAT IS IT? A flavorful fried base made with tomatoes, onions, ají peppers, garlic, herbs, and spices, adding depth to many dishes. Salt pork is often an addition.

TASTE: Varies depending on the recipe, but generally savory and garlicky, with a hint of sweetness from the peppers.

USAGE: Used as a flavor base in stews, soups, sauces, and marinades.

SUBSTITUTIONS: Sofrito (page 38).

Sweet Plantain

WHAT IS IT? Ripe plantains with yellow and black skin. Can be purchased fresh or frozen.

TASTE: Sweet, tangy, caramelized, with a subtle banana flavor.

USAGE: Fried, candied, or baked. Used as a side for savory dishes or in desserts.

SUBSTITUTIONS: Ripe bananas.

Tamarind

WHAT IS IT? A brown hard-shelled pod containing tart, sticky pulp.

TASTE: Tart, sour, with a slightly smoky undertone.

USAGE: Used in stews, sauces, and dips, sometimes as a candy.

SUBSTITUTIONS: Lime juice with brown sugar, tamarind concentrate.

Tamarind Paste

WHAT IS IT? A dark paste made from tamarind pulp, often sold in jars or blocks.

TASTE: A concentrated sour and fruity flavor with hints of sweetness. Can sometimes be salty, depending on the brand.

USAGE: Used in marinades, sauces, and beverages.

SUBSTITUTIONS: Tamarind concentrate.

Yautía

WHAT IS IT? A white-fleshed root vegetable with hairy dark brown bark-like skin; aka malanga.

TASTE: Slightly nutty, starchy, similar to cassava.

USAGE: Boiled, mashed, fried, or used in stews and soups.

SUBSTITUTIONS: Cassava, taro, potatoes.

Yuca

WHAT IS IT? A starchy root vegetable, also known as cassava.

TASTE: Neutral, slightly sweet, earthy when cooked.

USAGE: Boiled, mashed, fried, grated for fritters, or used in stews and soups.

SUBSTITUTIONS: Potatoes, taro, yautía.

Yuca Starch

WHAT IS IT? A naturally gluten-free starch extracted from the yuca (cassava) root. Also known as tapioca starch.

TASTE: Very mild and neutral, with a faint sweetness.

USAGE: Used to thicken stews, soups, and sauces without clouding them and to give baked goods a chewy, stretchy texture.

SUBSTITUTIONS: Corn starch or potato starch.

Part One

A Puerto
Gets Los

Rican

I should have known our marriage was doomed. We got hitched in front of an Elvis impersonator. That doesn't scream, "This is going to last forever." Still, I'm dumbstruck when I find my husband's account on Ashley Maddison, a dating website for married people who want to have affairs. His screen name is AwesomePants007. He left his profile open on my computer, probably after clicking "Remember me always" in the browser. That is neither awesome nor 007-ish.

I try to make it work, but there is no going back. I file for divorce. I'm devastated. I don't recognize the person staring back at me in the bathroom mirror. She is gaunt, hollow, empty. She has disappeared inside a life of her own design.

I foolishly buy tickets for my two-year-old son and me to fly to Puerto Rico and visit my family. It's a chunk of money I shouldn't put on my credit card, but I'm not in my right mind, and I miss the island terribly. It's been seventeen years since I've set foot on my homeland's soil. I need to go back to the beginning, back to a place before I was a mother and a wife. I need to remember who I am and where I come from.

I'm frayed, and I don't have the energy to tell my story over and over again to my family. But *mis tías* (my aunts) could sense it. Like many women, they've had a man try to break them. Instead of barraging me with a wall of questions, instinctively, they feed me. I devour everything in sight: smashed green plantain *tostones* so fresh from the frying pan I burn my fingertips as I dip them into a small bowl of mayo-ketchup; *chuletas can-can*, unctuous deep fried porkchops with crispy crackling skin, smothered in pungent *ajilimójili* garlic sauce; mounds of fluffy white rice scented with garlic and drowned in *habichuelas guisadas,* a brothy pink bean stew. The grassy aroma of *recao* (a fresh herb) intermingled with tangy tomato sauce wallops me. I blink back tears. This is a language I understand. Food as comfort. Food as memory. Food as healing. I'm being stitched back together by flavors, textures, and smells.

I visit the remains of my childhood home, the defunct dairy farm where my abuelo and abuela, my father's parents, raised me and my twin brother. When we were five, a fire gobbled up our farmhouse and left a charred cement foundation in its place, like a dirty plate where a beautiful meal had once been placed. We lost everything: my abuela's recipe box, family photos, even our beloved pets. I watch my son run back and forth across the foundation, looking so much like my brother had those thirty some odd years ago. I'm lost in my earliest memories.

I remember buttery steam rising from a golden mound of cornmeal dough as my Abuela Dora taught me how to shape *sorullos*. I'm engulfed in the recollection of the thunderous crunch of that cornmeal fritter. It had come straight out of the pot of bubbling oil that had a permanent residency on our stove. The earthy golden crust gave way to a creamy filling made nutty with Edam cheese. I reached for a second one before I finished chewing the first.

About twice a week, my abuela took my brother and me to the fishing village a mile away. It was our habit to trail behind her as she shopped for snapper. I gobbled up the sight of men with stained hands folding nets and cleaning buckets. The smell of gasoline from a boat's motor intermingled with that of the fresh catch. Abuela Dora stopped to talk to a lady who sold blistered salty bacalaítos, giant codfish fritters bigger than our faces. We pestered her for the greasy treat, and she hissed back at us, *"No jodan. Hay mucho que hacer."* ("Don't fuss around. There's work to be done.") She bought one for each of us while she continued with her *bochinche* (gossip). That first briny bite, doughy yet crunchy and almost too hot to chew, led to a nonstop round of rapid-fire munching. Bacalaítos were always gone too soon. They left me jealous of the napkin that still held a few of their crispy crumbs.

My Abuelo Quique had a sweet tooth. He bought a box full of *pastelillos* every day, and every time he opened it, my heart raced in anticipation. They were made from puff pastry layered with silky cream cheese and tangy guava paste and dusted with so much powdered sugar it made me sneeze. He pulled the car over whenever he saw a street vendor selling bags of the powdery coconut candy known as *turrón de coco*. After buying it, he tore the white block covered in rainbow-colored sprinkles into chunks, crumbs falling all over the vinyl seat. "*Carajo*," he cursed quietly as he passed delicately brittle pieces to the back seat for my brother and me to nibble on. I loved how the candy melted gently in my mouth, like a creamy coconut fudge.

Even though there's nothing left to see, this farm is the foundation of who I am. It is the last place I felt a sense of unquestionable belonging. I realize it's not the loss of our possessions that haunts me, it's the aroma of saucy sofrito sizzling in my abuela's caldero, the glee of sharing *dulce de ajonjolí* (sesame candy) with my abuelo, the pure joy of the moments we shared around that small kitchen table. This is where my love of food began.

After the fire swallowed up everything we owned, my brother and I went to live with our mother in the posh suburb of Isla Verde in San Juan. She had left us in her husband's parents' care when we were just a few months old, and I only had a faint memory of her visiting us at the farm to give us a set of Big Wheels, which we pedaled for hours on our *marquesina* (patio). As she ushered us into her Mercedes, it felt like we were leaving with a stranger.

She was a gorgeous, cinnamon-skinned twenty-four-year-old Colombian woman. Everything about her was big: her long afro, her throaty laugh, and her lightning-quick temper. What I remember most from those first weeks is finding her in the kitchen in the early mornings. She stood over a pan of eggs scrambled with green onions and tomatoes, Colombian *huevos pericos*. She wore a short silky white robe, held a spatula in one hand and a Benson & Hedges 100 in the other. From what I could tell, she was happiest in that small room, listening to her music on blast and dancing between stirs.

I watched her intently as we ate, as if she were one of those puzzles where you search for words hidden in a grid of letters. I tried to figure her out as she told tales of her poverty-stricken childhood in Colombia. She was one of six kids, and it was her chore to buy a liter of milk for the family every morning. She giggled as she confessed to drinking half of the milk on the way home and refilling the bottle with water. Moments like these made me feel closer to her, though they were rare. Her social calendar was booked solid, so we spent many days at her mother's tenement apartment in Bayamón.

Whenever I was around her, I could not take my eyes off my Abuela Alicia. Unlike my Abuela Dora, who had short white hair and never wore makeup, Alicia dyed her hair jet black and wore tons of mascara and red lipstick. She puffed on Benson & Hedges 100s while she taught my brother and me how to chew Chiclets, square pieces of white gum that she purchased from the corner store. She taught us to crush them with our back teeth and then demanded we spit them out after a minute of furious chomping. She gave us quarters to buy glazed donuts from a man who sold them out of a beat-up white truck and *limbers*, frozen juices sold in plastic cups, from the lady across the hall, who always seemed to have her short hair wound tightly in pink rollers. We passed her the quarter through the wrought iron of her front door, and she reached into her *neverita* (cooler) to hand us the frozen block of tamarind juice, never once leaving her seat. It took us almost thirty minutes to power through the ice, sucking out the sweet and sour juice until we were almost dizzy, then sipping on the lightly flavored water as what was left of the limber melted slowly in the cup.

I don't remember my Abuela Alicia ever sitting down for a meal, but it seemed she was always making a pot of *café colao*. She'd stand over a pot of boiling water, stirring in coffee grounds with a soup spoon, which she then strained through what looked like a sock, but I realize now was a reusable coffee filter.

As we waited for the coffee to seep through, she told me harrowing tales of El Cuco, a crazed, snarling beast who ate misbehaving children. For the uninitiated, he's like the Boogeyman but with a higher murder rate. Abuela Alicia said I had to be alert because he lived in the hallway outside her apartment. I stared at my reflection in the toaster, terrified.

It hits me now that El Cuco comes in many shapes and sizes throughout life. Sometimes, he's a fire that eats everything in its path; other times, his screen name is Awesomepants007.

The healing through food started a few weeks after my return to Seattle from my stay in Puerto Rico. I wanted to feel like myself again, to taste the flavors that made up the core of who I was. It began with a sprinkle of adobo on my roast chicken. Then came a sofrito base for tomato soup. Before I knew it, I found myself in the produce section of H Mart, an Asian supermarket, looking for recao to throw in my beef stew. I almost wept when I found it and held it to my nose. I felt seen.

Foundations and Then Some

Spice Blends and Savory Sauces

ADOBO

MAKES A GENEROUS ¼ CUP

- 2 tablespoons kosher salt
- ½ teaspoon freshly ground black pepper
- 1 tablespoon onion powder
- 1 tablespoon garlic powder
- 1 teaspoon ground oregano
- 2 teaspoons ground cumin
- ½ teaspoon ground turmeric

It's rare to find a Puerto Rican kitchen without a bottle of adobo in it. My Abuela Dora kept hers next to the stove. She would yell for my brother and me to behave, shaking a dash into her beans as an exclamation point after every syllable. *"¡Se callan o los callo!"* ("Shut up, or I'll shut you up!")

This garlicky all-purpose seasoning blend is used in most savory preparations on the island and in the diaspora. You can also use it as a dry rub on any of your favorite proteins and sprinkle it into soups, sauces, and stews to instantly boost flavor.

In an airtight container, use a fork to stir together the salt, pepper, onion powder, garlic powder, oregano, cumin, and turmeric. Seal and store in a cool, dark place for up to 3 months.

SAZÓN

Sazón is more than a spice. It's a vibe. Bad Bunny (one of the biggest musical artists ever and a proud Puerto Rican) might say it best: *"Ahora todos quieren ser latinos, pero les falta sazón."* ("Now everyone wants to be Latino, but they're missing sazón.")

Sazón takes flavors over the top, makes you pause, makes you go *mmmmm*. The all-purpose spice blend is a foundational flavor of Puerto Rican cuisine. Its base is annatto, which adds a grounding earthiness to sauces, grains, and proteins, and a golden color to everything it touches. Think of it as a Boricua's Midas Touch. (Boricua is what we Puerto Ricans call ourselves, honoring the Indigenous name for our island, Borikén.)

MAKES A BIT LESS THAN ¼ CUP

2 teaspoons garlic powder

1 teaspoon ground oregano

2 teaspoons ground cumin

2 teaspoons ground coriander

2 teaspoons ground annatto

1 teaspoon ground turmeric

In a clean 4-ounce jar, combine the garlic powder, oregano, cumin, coriander, annatto, and turmeric. Seal and store in a cool, dry place for up to 2 months.

RECAÍTO

Recaíto is the foundation of Puerto Rican sofrito; the names are often used interchangeably. *Sofrito* means "to fry," so once recaíto hits the pan along with other ingredients (like annatto oil, tomato sauce, and salt pork), it becomes sofrito. Recaíto gets its name from its main ingredient, an herb called *recao*. The "*ito*" is a suffix that Puerto Ricans add to many words, like a linguistic chef's kiss. This puree of herbs and aromatics brings a grassy earthiness to many of our dishes. I keep it on hand to add to grains, soups, sauces, braises, and stews.

Traditionally, we use *ají dulce* peppers to make recaíto in Puerto Rico. Because they can be mission impossible to come by in the Lower 48, a subtly sweet red bell pepper is a solid substitute. Cubanelle peppers aren't always available at local markets. In those instances, I reach for a green bell pepper. Look for recao at Latino or Asian grocery stores, where it might be called culantro, Mexican coriander, long coriander, sawtooth coriander, or ngò gai. It has long, serrated leaves that smell like pungent cilantro. If you can't find it, substitute it with one bunch of cilantro stems. Will it taste the same? Nope. But it will be close enough. And when you're Spanglish, close enough can still feel like you're back at your abuela's table.

You can use a fresh batch right away and store leftovers in an airtight container in the refrigerator for up to two weeks, or freeze it in ice cube trays and transfer the cubes to an airtight container where they will keep for up to four months. Defrost before using. If you're not scared of a bit of splatter, throw the frozen cubes in a hot pan with a touch of oil. They'll break up quickly.

MAKES ABOUT 4 CUPS

3 tablespoons olive oil

8 large garlic cloves, coarsely chopped (about ¼ cup)

1 medium yellow onion, coarsely chopped

2 Cubanelle peppers, stemmed, seeded, and coarsely chopped

1 red bell pepper, stemmed, seeded, and coarsely chopped

1 large bunch cilantro, rinsed, leaves and tender stems coarsely chopped

1 large bunch recao, coarsely chopped (may substitute stems from the above cilantro)

1. In a food processor, combine the olive oil and garlic, pulsing until the garlic is finely chopped. Add the onion, Cubanelle peppers, and red bell pepper; pulse just long enough to form a chunky salsa. Add the cilantro and recao. Puree until fairly smooth, scraping down the bowl as needed.

2. Transfer to an airtight container, seal, and store as directed in the headnote.

ANNATTO OIL

Over the years, annatto oil destroyed my Abuela Dora's sandy beige Formica kitchen counter, leaving orange-hued stains that couldn't be scrubbed off with mountains of Ajax and a steady stream of softly mumbled curses. But, in my humble opinion, the deep earthy notes it imparts are worth a few blemishes. This powerful ingredient is also known as achiote oil because it's made with the seeds of the achiote tree, which is native to Puerto Rico. Some cheesemakers use annatto to give cheddar its orange color. Boricuas use it to add a golden hue and citrusy, peppery notes to many foods, including rice, pasteles, and empanadilla dough. It can also lend a deep reddish-brown color to roasted chicken or pork. But be warned: it will stain anything porous, so be careful!

MAKES 1 CUP

1 cup vegetable or canola oil

¼ cup annatto seeds

1. In a small heavy saucepan, over medium heat, combine the vegetable oil and annatto seeds. Once the mixture begins to make a little noise, reduce the heat to low. Cook for 7 to 10 minutes, stirring a few times (with a metal spoon) to keep the seeds from sticking. During that time, small bubbles will appear on the surface and the oil will pick up the seeds' color. Remove from the heat.

2. Cool to room temperature then pour through a fine-mesh strainer into an airtight container, discarding the seeds. Seal and store for up to 1 week in a cool, dry place, or refrigerate for up to 1 month.

SOFRITO

MAKES ⅔ CUP

- 1 tablespoon Annatto Oil (page 37)
- Scant 1 ounce salt pork, minced (2 heaping tablespoons; may substitute pancetta or bacon)
- ½ cup Recaíto (page 34)
- 1 teaspoon dried oregano
- ¼ cup tomato paste (may substitute ½ cup fresh tomato puree or plain tomato sauce)

I'm not exaggerating when I say that sofrito has supernatural powers. I've seen it bring the most obnoxiously loud-mouthed guests to a standstill—the importance of telling their extravagant stories trumped by its garlicky aroma permeating the room. Ingesting sofrito brings Boricuas back to a time and place; different for all of us but home to each of us.

The word *sofrito* references the frying of a sauce, a technique brought to the island by Spanish colonizers. In Puerto Rico, sofrito is made when you add recaíto to a hot pan that's been greased with a little annatto oil and rendered salt pork. You then add spices and some form of tomato. Some people use freshly pureed tomatoes; others use tomato sauce. I prefer tomato paste for its concentrated flavor and because it keeps the sofrito tight. Frying the sauce deepens flavors and creates the kind of aroma that will have everyone in your home exclaiming, "It smells so good in here!"

Every Boricua family has its version of sofrito. Card-carrying members of the "food police" will insist there is only one right way to make it. I disagree. The beauty of cooking is getting the opportunity to create, don't let a few missing traditional ingredients keep you from connecting to your roots and don't hesitate to use nontraditional ingredients that you love. Use what you have and make this recipe your own.

Sofrito has a pungent, herbaceous flavor that is rounded out by the fat of the salt pork. Like fish sauce, it's ridiculously strong on its own. Think of sofrito as a big-picture ingredient. It adds backbone to anything it's incorporated in. Use it as the first step when you're making soups, beans, stews, and braises—as well as my Lamb Picadillo Meatloaf (page 142). To keep this recipe vegan, substitute the salt pork with plant-based bacon or 1 heaping teaspoon of white miso paste.

1. In a medium saucepan, heat the Annatto Oil over medium heat. Once it begins to shimmer, add the salt pork. Cook for 3 to 5 minutes, stirring a few times to keep it from sticking, until its fat has rendered and the pork is golden and crisped. Reduce the heat as needed to keep the fat and oil from smoking.

2. Stir in the Recaíto, oregano, and tomato paste. Cook for about 3 minutes, stirring, or until the Sofrito is evenly blended and thickened. Refrigerate in an airtight container for up to 1 week, or portion it in ice cube trays and freeze for up to 3 months.

PIQUE

MAKES 2 CUPS

- 1½ cups distilled white vinegar
- ½ cup pineapple juice, preferably fresh
- 1 teaspoon granulated sugar
- 1 tablespoon kosher salt
- 6 serrano peppers, stemmed and cut in half lengthwise
- 4 red bird's-eye (Thai) chile peppers, stemmed and cut in half lengthwise
- 2 Scotch bonnet chile peppers, stemmed and cut in half from top to bottom (may substitute habañeros)
- One 1 x 4-inch strip of lime zest (no pith)
- 6 garlic cloves, smashed
- Small knob of fresh turmeric, smashed
- 5 whole black peppercorns

Contrary to popular belief, Puerto Ricans don't use many hot peppers in their cooking. Instead, our favorite flavor is *agridulce*, or savory-sweet. But, of course, there are always exceptions to the rule, and that's where pique comes in. You'll find this vinegar-based hot sauce on most Boricua tables; everyone has their own version. It's used in the same way you would use any hot sauce, to add a little fire to savory preparations.

Traditionally, pique is made with ají caballero, a tiny hot pepper that grows abundantly on the island. But most grocery stores on the big continent don't carry this beauty, so Spanglish-it-up and substitute it with your favorite hot pepper. You can leave the peppers whole, but I prefer to cut them in half lengthwise to give the vinegar access to all those extra-hot seeds!

For optimal results, let your pique ferment in a sunny spot for at least a few days. If you need some right away, add the vinegar, pineapple juice, sugar, and salt to a small pot and bring them to a simmer. Then, take it off the heat and add the rest of the ingredients, giving them a quick pickle.

Sometimes, garlic turns a blueish green in vinegar. Don't be alarmed; it's just enzymes having a chemical reaction to the acidity. Blue garlic is still perfectly edible. The color of the serranos might dull a bit in the vinegar, but the bird's-eye and Scotch bonnet peppers will remain vibrant. As you go through the pique, don't hesitate to refill the bottle with more vinegar and peppers. It's okay to add them to the old batch!

Pique is vinegar-based and can last indefinitely in the fridge, though I keep mine at room temperature.

1. In a clean a 1-quart, wide-mouthed jar, combine the vinegar, pineapple juice, sugar, and salt, stirring until the sugar and salt have dissolved.

2. Add the serrano, bird's-eye, and Scotch bonnet peppers, the lime zest, garlic, turmeric, and peppercorns, stirring to distribute them evenly. Make sure the peppers are completely submerged.

3. Seal and let stand at room temperature in a sunny spot from 3 days to 3 weeks to allow the flavor to develop. Afterward, refrigerate (to keep it from intensifying further) for up to 1 month.

SPICY MAYO-KETCHUP

This is Puerto Rican fry sauce, and we use it as a tasty dip for many of our *frituras* (fried goods), such as tostones and sorullitos. There's beauty in the simplicity of mayo-ketchup. The condiment is tangy with a touch of sweetness—a perfect example of the savory-sweet flavors Boricuas love. Traditionally, it's just a blend of two parts mayo and one part ketchup, but I like to add a little heat and acidity with chopped Calabrian chiles and their liquid. Fish sauce and garlic add depth.

If you watched my season of *MasterChef*, it might surprise you that I use fish sauce in this recipe. You might remember me staring aghast into a camera during a Mystery Box Challenge and asking, "What is fish sauce? And why does it taste like death?" Long story short, I had received a bottle of fish sauce to cook with in that challenge and I was unfamiliar with the ingredient. So, I filled a tablespoon with it, put the whole thing in my mouth to taste it, and proceeded to sputter, gasp, and choke, much to the delight of the camera crew.

While I do not recommend drinking fish sauce by the spoonful, a few drops are pure magic. They add a joyous depth to mayo-ketchup. If you're vegetarian, use a plant-based mayo and skip the fish sauce. Use a ¼ teaspoon of white miso instead.

MAKES ABOUT ½ CUP

¼ cup mayonnaise

2 tablespoons ketchup

1 teaspoon minced Calabrian chiles (jarred), plus 2 teaspoons of their liquid

⅛ teaspoon fish sauce

1 garlic clove, Microplaned into a paste

1. In a small airtight container, stir together the mayo, ketchup, chiles and the liquid, the fish sauce, and garlic until well blended (and a little soupy).

2. Use right away, or seal and refrigerate for up to 2 weeks.

ESCABECHE

Escabeche is a preservation technique, key on an island where electricity falters daily. But it's also a ridiculously delicious sauce. This tangy pickling liquid was one of my mother's favorites. She used to pour it over boiled yuca and eat whatever was left over at the bottom of the bowl with a soup spoon. Use it with Scalloped Viandas with Escabeche (page 127) or drizzle it over my recipe for Plantain Chip–Breaded Chicken Nuggets (page 96).

MAKES ABOUT 3 CUPS

1 cup olive oil

2 small yellow onions, cut into ¼-inch-thick rings

6 garlic cloves, thinly sliced

¼ teaspoon kosher salt

3 bay leaves

½ teaspoon black peppercorns

⅓ cup distilled white vinegar

1. In a heavy pot, heat the olive oil over medium-low heat until it shimmers. Stir in the onions and cook for 5 to 7 minutes, until they become translucent and softened but have not yet taken on any color.

2. Add the garlic, salt, bay leaves, peppercorns, and vinegar and cook for 3 to 4 minutes, stirring, until everything has warmed through. Remove from the heat once the onions are tender, about 10 minutes.

3. Let the escabeche steep until it has cooled, about 20 minutes. Store in an airtight, nonreactive container for up to 1 week. Keep the bay leaves in the mixture and discard them before serving.

AJILIMÓJILI

MAKES ABOUT 3 CUPS

This punchy fresh pepper and garlic sauce is the ride-or-die condiment for many Puerto Rican fritters, aka frituras. You'll find it served next to tostones or *arañitas* (shredded green plantain patties) in a small bowl or (like my abuela kept hers) in a squeeze bottle with a tapered top that has a hole the size of a #2 pencil. Chunky with a powerful acidity that cuts through fat, this is also often served over grilled meats, and seafood. Fish sauce is not a traditional ingredient, but a dash of it deepens the powers of this sauce, so why not? It is next to impossible to source the traditional ají peppers and recao used to make this sauce stateside, but if you can find them, use them instead of the sweet peppers and cilantro. Though often made with tomatoes, I keep my Spanglish version green and really lean in to the grassiness and sweetness of the peppers. Feel free to adjust the amount of habañeros to your heat preference. I use this sauce to make a quick and spicy Bucatini with Clams Ajilimójili (page 140) and it is absolutely divine!

- 1 cup extra-virgin olive oil, divided
- 1 small yellow onion, coarsely chopped
- 6 small sweet peppers, stemmed, seeded, and coarsely chopped
- 1 Cubanelle pepper, stemmed, seeded, and coarsely chopped
- 4 habañero peppers, stemmed, seeded, and coarsely chopped
- ¼ cup distilled white vinegar
- ¼ cup fresh lime juice
- 1 bunch cilantro, leaves and tender stems, coarsely chopped
- 8 garlic cloves, minced
- 1¼ teaspoons kosher salt
- ¼ teaspoon freshly ground black pepper
- ¼ teaspoon dried oregano
- ¼ teaspoon ground cumin
- Dash of fish sauce

1. In a skillet, warm ¼ cup of the olive oil over medium heat. Add the onion, sweet peppers, Cubanelle pepper, and habañero peppers. Sauté for 3 to 5 minutes, until the onion and peppers have softened.
2. In a blender, combine the remaining olive oil, vinegar, lime juice, cilantro, garlic, salt, black pepper, oregano, cumin, and the dash of fish sauce. Puree until smooth and uniformly green.
3. Working in batches as needed, add the softened peppers and onion. Pulse until a coarse, chunky sauce forms.
4. Transfer to an airtight container and refrigerate for up to 3 days or freeze for up to 3 months.

SALSA CRIOLLA

You'll find salsa criolla blanketing many classic Puerto Rican dishes. This versatile sauce is made with tomatoes, olives, onions, and peppers, and can be poured over mofongo, used to braise chicken, and made into a base for Salsa Criolla Shakshuka (page 66).

MAKES ABOUT 2¼ CUPS

2 tablespoons olive oil

1 small yellow onion, cut in half and then into ¼-inch-thick quarter moons

Kosher salt

1 Cubanelle pepper, stemmed, seeded, and cut into thin 2-inch-long slices (may substitute banana pepper or green bell pepper)

2 garlic cloves, minced

¼ cup Sofrito (page 38)

1 tablespoon tomato paste

1 cup (8 ounces) crushed tomatoes and their juices

¼ cup alcaparrado, store-bought, finely chopped (see Note)

1 bay leaf

1. In a small heavy pot, heat the olive oil over medium heat until it has warmed through. Add the onion and season with salt to taste. Cook gently for about 3 minutes, or until translucent.

2. Add the Cubanelle pepper and the garlic; cook for about 2 minutes, or until the pepper pieces soften and the garlic becomes fragrant. Stir in the Sofrito and tomato paste; cook for about 5 minutes, or until the sauce has thickened and darkened in color.

3. Add the crushed tomatoes and their juices, the alcaparrado, and bay leaf. Reduce the heat to medium-low and cook for about 15 minutes, stirring a few times, or until the sauce thickens further. Taste, and add more salt as needed. Discard the bay leaf before serving or storing. Refrigerate in an airtight container for up to 3 days or freeze for up to 3 months.

NOTE: Alcaparrado is a mix of small, green Spanish olives (aka Manzanilla) and tiny capers. The pitted olives are stuffed with small strips of roasted red pepper. The ratio of olives to capers is typically 3:1.

CILANTRO CREMA

This dressing is earthy, tangy, creamy, and lip-smacking good. The mint is not a traditional ingredient, but it is fantastic. I like to make a batch and drizzle this over fresh avocado, simple salads, and fried eggs. It also pairs perfectly with tacos, rice bowls, and fried chicken.

MAKES ABOUT 1 CUP

- 1 (packed) cup cilantro leaves (see Note)
- ¼ cup mint leaves
- ¼ cup full-fat sour cream
- ¼ cup unsweetened coconut cream
- ⅛ teaspoon peeled, finely grated ginger root
- Finely grated zest and juice of 1 lime
- ¼ teaspoon garlic salt
- Pinch of freshly ground black pepper
- Pinch of ground cumin

NOTE: Don't toss the cilantro stems; keep them in a freezer-safe container and use them to make Recaíto (page 34).

1. In a blender, combine the cilantro, mint, sour cream, coconut cream, ginger, lime juice, garlic salt, the pinch of black pepper, and the pinch of cumin. Puree until smooth. Taste for seasoning and adjust to your preference.

2. Transfer to a serving bowl, then stir in the lime zest. Use right away or refrigerate in an airtight container for up to 5 days.

TAMARIND GUAVA BBQ SAUCE

Did you know Puerto Ricans invented BBQ? Well, sort of. Our native Taíno people created the first framework of sticks to smoke roasted meats and called it *barbacoa*. Solid BBQ is nothing without a mop or sauce and this one is my favorite. There's tang from the tamarind, a hint of sweetness from the guava, and a touch of heat from the pique. I use it as a glaze on Tamarind Roast Chicken (page 145), beef ribs, and pork chops. Try using on roasted carrots or as a sauce for tofu. Or mix it into pulled chicken or pork for the best BBQ sandwiches. Add it as a base for pizza and wraps, too. It's just that good!

MAKES A GENEROUS 2 CUPS

- 2 tablespoons fresh lime juice
- 1 cup chicken stock or broth
- ½ cup guava paste, cut into a small dice (see Tip)
- ½ cup tamarind paste concentrate
- 2 tablespoons tomato paste
- 2 tablespoons Pique (page 41), or other hot sauce
- 1 teaspoon soy sauce
- 1 teaspoon Worcestershire sauce
- 1 teaspoon Adobo (page 30)
- 1 teaspoon Sazón (page 33)
- 1 teaspoon light or dark brown sugar
- Kosher salt and freshly ground black pepper

1. In a small heavy saucepan, over medium heat, combine the lime juice, stock, guava paste, and tamarind paste. As the mixture heats through, break down the guava and tamarind by using a sturdy spoon to press them against the sides of the pan as you stir.

2. Once the guava and tamarind have dissolved, add the tomato paste, Pique, soy sauce, Worcestershire sauce, Adobo, Sazón, and light brown sugar. Raise the heat to medium-high and bring to a boil, then reduce the heat to medium-low and cook for 10 minutes, or until thickened.

3. Cool, then season with salt and pepper to taste. Transfer to an airtight container and refrigerate for up to 1 week or freeze for up to 3 months.

TIP: Brush a little neutral oil (like canola or grapeseed) on your knife blade so the guava paste doesn't stick to it as you dice it.

PASSION FRUIT VINAIGRETTE

When I was growing up, there was a passion fruit vine just outside of my Abuela Dora's home. When the vine was flowering, I loved the scent so much that I'd inhale big gulps of air as I left or entered the house, much to my abuela's chagrin. While you do not have to be as (to quote my grandmother) *"exagerada"* (exaggerated) as me, I do recommend that you smell your passion fruit before purchasing them. If they are fragrant, have wrinkled skin, give a little when gently pressed, and feel heavy for their size, they are ripe. You can also skip the hunt for perfectly ripe passion fruit altogether and use frozen.

This dressing is an absolute delight, easy to make, and fantastic on leafy greens or sliced avocados. Drizzle it on sandwiches and wraps, or add it to a little sour cream to create a flavorful dip.

MAKES A LITTLE LESS THAN 1 CUP

Pulp from 2 ripe passion fruit, or ¼ cup frozen/defrosted passion fruit pulp

½ cup olive oil

1 tablespoon fresh lime juice, plus more as needed

2 tablespoons champagne vinegar, plus more as needed (may substitute rice vinegar or sherry vinegar)

2 tablespoons honey, plus more as needed

½ teaspoon kosher salt, plus more as needed

1. In a clean pint jar, combine the passion fruit pulp, olive oil, lime juice, vinegar, honey, and salt. Seal and shake to form an emulsified vinaigrette.

2. Taste and adjust the flavor to your liking with more lime juice, vinegar, honey, and/or salt. Refrigerate in an airtight container for up to 2 weeks.

Things to Eat Earlier in the Day

Eggs, Sweetbreads, and Breakfast Treats

PAN DE BONO SKILLET PANCAKE

Pancakes were my earliest solo kitchen endeavor. I was a latchkey kid at age six, meaning that if I wanted an after-school snack, I had to make it. So I grabbed the family-size box of the just-add-water mix that was a mainstay in our cupboard, and cooked pancakes for my twin brother and me. We doused them with syrup and ate a stack while we watched *Scooby Doo, Where Are You!* and *Donahue*. That's how we learned English, too—in front of that TV, eating pancakes, trying to figure out what the lady next to the gray-haired man with the microphone was so upset about.

This Pan de Bono Skillet Pancake is my grown-up version of those snacking pancakes. Pan de Bono is a gluten-free cheese bread from my mother's homeland of Colombia. So think of this as a cheese-bread skillet pancake even your gluten-free friends can enjoy.

I serve it with Banana Butter-Rum Sauce (page 172), which is inspired by the bananas I'd fry in butter to top our after-school pancakes in case we (gasp!) ran out of syrup. You can, of course, omit the sauce and serve this skillet pancake with syrup, honey, whipped cream, confectioners' sugar, or fresh berries.

SERVES 4

- 4 tablespoons (½ stick) salted butter
- ¼ cup whole milk, plus more as needed
- 1 cup queso fresco, crumbled or cut into chunks
- 1 cup Cotija cheese
- 2 large eggs
- 1 cup yuca starch
- ⅔ cup Masarepa cornmeal
- 1 teaspoon baking powder
- ½ teaspoon baking soda
- 2 teaspoons granulated sugar
- ⅛ teaspoon kosher salt
- Powdered sugar, for serving (optional)
- Candied papaya, for serving (optional)

1. Preheat the oven to 400°F.
2. Melt the butter in a 10-inch, oven-proof skillet (cast iron is perfect), on the middle oven rack.
3. Meanwhile, in a food processor, combine the milk, queso fresco, and Cotija cheese. Puree to form a smooth batter. Add the eggs, one by one, combining after each addition. If the batter is dry, add more milk, tablespoon by tablespoon, until a thick batter forms.
4. In a small bowl, mix the yuca starch, Masarepa cornmeal, baking powder, baking soda, granulated sugar, and salt. Add to the food processor and pulse until a dough forms.
5. Open the oven just long enough to check the butter; it should be melted. Carefully swirl it around to coat the sides of the skillet, then quickly pour the butter over the dough. Pulse to incorporate. Press the dough into the greased skillet. Bake for 18 to 20 minutes, until the pancake turns light golden brown and crisped at the edges.
6. Cool for a few minutes before cutting your skillet pancake into wedges, and serve warm with whatever your heart desires. I love it dusted with a little powdered sugar or served with slices of candied papaya.

ANNATTO BISCUITS

I fell in love with biscuits from my first bite at my Texas elementary school breakfast. I was obsessed with the dusty tops that left grains of flour on my fingertips and the way they steamed as I tucked butter between the halves. When the liquid gold inevitably drizzled through my fingers onto my wrist, I'd lick it off with glee.

This dough gets its golden hue and earthiness from annatto, one of the most important spices in Puerto Rican cuisine. The addition of orange zest adds depth and very subtle citrus notes.

These are fantastic on their own served with a pat of butter and Guanabana Quick Jam (page 166). You can also serve drizzled with Butifarra Gravy (page 61) to create a colorful riff on Southern-style biscuits and gravy.

MAKES 12 BISCUITS

- 1½ cups heavy cream, plus more for brushing
- ⅓ cup annatto seeds
- 1 strip of orange zest from a fresh orange (1-inch wide x 3-inches long, no pith)
- 2 cups sifted and chilled all-purpose flour, plus up to ½ cup for dusting
- 1½ tablespoons baking powder
- ¾ teaspoon kosher salt
- 8 tablespoons (1 stick) frozen salted butter, plus 2 tablespoons (¼ stick) melted

TIP: **To chill annatto cream faster, pour it into a lasagna pan or other large, high-sided baking dish, and cool it down in the freezer while you make the dough. Do not let it firm up.**

1. In a small saucepan, heat the heavy cream over medium heat, just until barely bubbling at the edges. Remove from the heat and stir in the annatto seeds and strip of orange zest.

2. Infuse for 20 minutes, then strain through a fine-mesh strainer into a container, discarding the solids. It should be a pale orange in color. Cover and refrigerate until well chilled.

3. In a mixing bowl, whisk together the 2 cups flour, the baking powder, and salt. Using the large-hole side of a box grater, grate the stick of butter into the bowl. Using a fork to quickly toss it together, make sure all the butter pieces are coated. (If needed, cover and refrigerate this mixture until your annatto cream is thoroughly chilled.)

4. Make a well in the middle of the flour/butter mixture and add the chilled annatto cream. Using a fork or spatula to work it in, gently shape the mixture into a shaggy dough.

5. Use some of the remaining ½ cup flour to lightly dust your work surface. Transfer the dough there and sprinkle it with more flour. Lightly flour your rolling pin and use it to roll out the dough to a 9 x 5 x 1-inch rectangle, with the short sides parallel to the edge of your work surface.

6. Fold the dough over itself toward the center (in thirds), like a business letter. Give the dough a quarter turn and gently roll it again into a 9 x 5-inch rectangle. Repeat the process 2 more times. The dough will come together further as you work; pieces of butter should still be visible. Wrap the slab of dough in plastic wrap and refrigerate for at least 20 minutes and up to 2 days.

Continues

7. When ready to bake, preheat the oven to 400°F. Line a baking sheet with parchment paper or a silicone liner.

8. Flour your work surface, as needed. Unwrap the dough and gently roll it out to a rectangle that is 1 inch thick. Using a 3½-inch round cutter, dip the cutter into some flour, and press straight down into the dough (no twisting) to create as many biscuits as you can. Re-roll the scraps to make a total of 12 biscuits.

9. Arrange them on the prepared baking sheet so their sides touch. Lightly brush the tops with a little heavy cream and bake for 15 to 20 minutes until golden. Serve warm.

BUTIFARRA GRAVY

If you've ever spent any time in the South, then you know gravy is a way of life. Though it wasn't something I grew up eating in San Juan, I consumed this velvety sauce many times a week during the years I lived in Atlanta. It was often served for breakfast drizzled over steaming hot biscuits, but also for lunch layered with slices of meatloaf or with fried chicken. It is rich, flavorful, and comforting.

This gravy recipe is made with *butifarra*, a typical pork sausage in Puerto Rico, first introduced by Spanish colonizers. It has a mild flavor that plays well with the buttery earthiness of my Annatto Biscuits (page 59). You can also drizzle this sauce on Lamb Picadillo Meatloaf (page 142) or over simply prepared mashed potatoes. If you can't find butifarra, substitute it with any other mildly-flavored pork sausage.

MAKES ABOUT 2¼ CUPS (ENOUGH FOR 12 BISCUITS)

- 12 ounces butifarra sausage, casings removed
- 3 tablespoons all-purpose flour
- 2 cups whole milk
- Pinch of freshly grated nutmeg
- Kosher salt and freshly ground black pepper
- 2 tablespoons finely chopped chives, for garnish

1. In a large saucepan, break up the sausage over medium heat, and cook for about 6 minutes—just until no trace of pink remains, taking care not to brown it. Break up any big clumps. Using a slotted spoon, transfer the sausage to a plate and pour off all but 2 tablespoons of its rendered fat in the pan.

2. Reduce the heat to medium-low. Sprinkle in the flour and whisk constantly to form a paste (roux); cook for about 1 minute, or until no traces of flour remain. Gradually whisk in the milk, add the nutmeg, and increase the heat to medium; don't stop whisking until the gravy thickens, about 5 minutes. Work your whisk into the round sides of the saucepan to dislodge any trapped flour to keep the gravy from getting lumpy.

3. Once the gravy is thick and glossy, stir in the cooked sausage. Taste and season with salt and pepper as needed. Keep warm or reheat before serving. Garnish with chives.

QUICHE PERICO
WITH LONGANIZA

My mother loved making huevos pericos. It's a very popular breakfast dish in her home country of Colombia and consists of eggs scrambled with chopped fresh tomato and thinly sliced green onions. I love the buttery texture of the eggs and the pops of tangy acidity from the tomato. For this recipe, I couldn't resist pairing the huevos pericos with Puerto Rican *longaniza* and making them into a quiche with a puff pastry crust. Because sometimes you have to be a little EXTRA.

Longaniza came to Puerto Rico by way of our Spanish colonizers. Traditionally, this sausage is stuffed with roughly chopped pork or chicken seasoned with annatto, garlic, oregano, salt, and pepper. This delicacy is so beloved in Puerto Rico there's a stretch of road dedicated to it called La Ruta de la Longaniza (The Longaniza Trail). Though I love this quiche with longaniza, you can substitute it with any mildly flavored sausage. If you're vegetarian, use a plant-based alternative. Your kitchen. Your rules.

SERVES 8

- 1 sheet (about 10 x 15-inches) frozen/defrosted puff pastry
- 6 ounces cured longaniza, cut into a small dice (about 1 cup)
- 1 to 2 scallions, thinly sliced on the diagonal (white and light-green parts)
- 1 garlic clove, minced
- ¼ cup grape tomato medley, thinly sliced
- 6 tablespoons cream cheese, at room temperature
- 5 large eggs, lightly beaten (9 eggs if you are using a deep-dish pie plate)
- ½ cup heavy cream (use 1 cup if you are using a deep-dish pie plate)
- ½ cup grated Parmigiano-Reggiano cheese
- Kosher salt and freshly ground black pepper
- Flat-leaf parsley leaves, for garnish

1. Preheat the oven to 425°F.
2. Using a rolling pin, roll out the puff pastry to a 12-inch square then transfer it to a 9-inch pie plate, trimming and crimping the edges as needed. Using a fork, prick the bottom a few times. Cover the dough with parchment paper, including the rim, and fill with pie weights (or dried beans or raw rice). Partially bake for about 20 minutes, or just until lightly golden. Cool for a few minutes, then remove the paper and weights. Using the fork again, prick a few holes in the parbaked bottom crust.
3. Reduce the oven temperature to 350°F.
4. In a heavy skillet, cook the longaniza over medium heat for 7 to 8 minutes until crisped. Using a slotted spoon, transfer it to a plate.
5. Add the scallions to the drippings left in the pan and cook for about 2 minutes, or until softened. Add the garlic and cook for about 1 minute, or until fragrant. Then add the tomatoes. Cook for about 2 minutes, or until softened.
6. In a mixing bowl, use a whisk to beat the cream cheese until smooth. Mix in the eggs, all but 1 tablespoon of the heavy cream, the Parmigiano-Reggiano, and all but 2 tablespoons of the crisped longaniza. Season with salt and pepper to taste.
7. Pour the filling into the parbaked crust. Scatter the reserved longaniza over the surface. Using a pastry brush, coat the crust's edges with the reserved heavy cream. Cover the edges with a pie-crust shield or make your own by forming a ring from a length of aluminum foil.
8. Bake for about 30 minutes, or until the crust is golden brown and the filling is set. Cool for at least 10 minutes before garnishing with parsley and serving.

GUAVA TOASTER TARTS
WITH CREAM CHEESE ICING

Our *finca* (farm) was in a very small beach town in Puerto Rico called Boquerón. The local *panadería* (bakery) was a few hundred feet from the entrance to our farmland, and my abuelo habitually pulled into the parking lot on his way back from running errands in the city.

It was my habit to stare, transfixed, at all the items in the pastry case for the entirety of the time it took my grandfather to place his order. It was a treasure box of confections, and I imagined its glow was identical to the one surrounding the baby Jesus.

He was obsessed with the *pastelillos de guayaba y queso* (guava and cheese pastries) that the bakery owners nestled between the *mantecaditos* (shortbread cookies) and *mallorcas* (sweet rolls). These turnovers are made of crispy puff pastry stuffed with guava paste and cream cheese. The combination is a love song, the fatty cream cheese supporting the tangy notes of guava paste like Patrick Swayze did Jennifer Gray in *Dirty Dancing*. (If you haven't watched that movie, I need you to put this book down and get your life straight.)

I was eight years old the first time I bit into a Pop-Tart, and my mind was blown! Sweet jam nestled between crispy crusts that you could warm in a toaster?! Genius! At the grocery store, I checked out all of the different flavors but never found the one I wanted: guava and cream cheese. So I created it. #Manifest

The convenience and consistency of store-bought pie dough is perfect for this recipe. You'll want to buy enough for a double-crust pie, and make sure to roll it out to an ⅛ inch thickness, or the ratio of crust to filling will be off.

MAKES 8 TARTS

- 1 store-bought double crust pie dough, chilled
- 1 egg white
- 1 cup guava jelly
- ⅛ teaspoon kosher salt
- 4 tablespoons cream cheese, at room temperature
- 4 tablespoons (½ stick) salted butter, at room temperature
- 1 cup confectioners' sugar
- 1 tablespoon heavy cream
- Finely grated zest of 1 orange

1. Place a rack in the center of your oven and preheat the oven to 450°F. Line two small baking sheets with parchment paper or silicone liners.

2. Unwrap the first half of the dough. Roll it about ⅛ inch thick. You want the dough to be thin, to keep the ratio of crust to filling balanced.

3. Cut the dough into eight 3 x 4-inch rectangles, rerolling scraps as needed. Place the rectangles on the prepared baking sheets and refrigerate while you roll out and cut the remaining dough. Once you have cut the second half of the dough into eight 3 x 4-inch rectangles, prick each one four times with a fork (to allow steam to escape). Keep these toward the center of the rectangle, spaced about a ½ inch apart.

Continues

4. To assemble, add 1 tablespoon water to the egg white and whisk together until slightly frothy. Use this egg wash to brush the perimeter of each rectangle of dough.

5. Spoon 2 tablespoons of guava jelly onto the middle of the undocked rectangles. Cover with the docked rectangles, so both of the egg washed perimeters are facing each other. Gently press the edges together, then use a fork to firmly seal the edges all around without puncturing the dough.

6. Brush all over with the egg wash. Bake for 20 to 25 minutes, until golden brown. Transfer the pastries to a wire rack to cool.

7. Make the icing: In a medium bowl, whisk together the kosher salt, cream cheese, butter, confectioners' sugar, and heavy cream, until smooth and creamy. Once the pastries have cooled, spread the icing over the center of each pastry and garnish with orange zest. Let the icing set before serving.

SALSA CRIOLLA SHAKSHUKA

This dish is gorgeous enough to score a starring role on your brunch table, yet easy enough for a quick weekday breakfast or even a weeknight dinner. The eggs simmer in a piquant tomato sauce loaded with herbaceous peppers, briny capers, and meaty olives. Garnish with creamy crumbled queso fresco and slices of earthy avocado for a ridiculously tasty finish. Serve it with slices of toasted bread rubbed with garlic, and dip away.

SERVES 6

- A double recipe of Salsa Criolla (page 49; about 4½ cups total)
- 6 large eggs
- Kosher salt
- 8 slices crusty bread, for serving
- 2 tablespoons olive oil
- 1 garlic clove, cut lengthwise in half
- Flesh of 1 ripe avocado, cut into half-moons, for garnish
- ½ cup (2 ounces) queso fresco, crumbled, for garnish
- Fresh cilantro leaves, for garnish
- Pique, for serving (page 41)

1. Position racks in the upper and lower thirds of the oven, then preheat the oven to 350°F.

2. In a 12-inch cast-iron or other oven-proof skillet, pour in your Salsa Criolla. Cook over medium heat for about 10 minutes, stirring a few times, or until the sauce has thickened further and no longer looks wet. Use the back of a large spoon to make a well in the sauce for each egg.

3. Crack 1 egg into a ramekin or small bowl, then pour it into a well in the Salsa Criolla. Repeat with the remaining eggs. Season all the eggs with salt to taste.

4. Cover the skillet then transfer it to the lower oven rack and bake for 3 or 5 minutes, until the egg whites become opaque and set.

5. Meanwhile, arrange the bread slices on a rimmed baking sheet. Brush the top with the olive oil and toast in the oven (upper rack) for 3 to 5 minutes, or until they slightly deepen in color (while the eggs are baking in the shakshuka). Rub the toasted sides of the bread with the cut garlic halves.

6. To serve, layer the avocado slices on the surface of the shakshuka. Scatter the queso fresco and cilantro over the top. Serve with the garlicky toasted bread and Pique.

Portugal

WHIPPED RICOTTA TOASTS WITH BITTER ORANGE JAM

We grew dozens of fruits and vegetables on our little ocean-front farm, and none were uglier than the *naranjas agrias*. The bitter orange's skin was a dull tangerine color, with splashes of lime green throughout, as if it had decided in the middle of its transformation that it didn't want to change colors after all. Its ridiculously bumpy texture was also an affront. It looked like the barnacle-encrusted rocks that lined our beach.

I wanted nothing to do with the naranja agria. So, of course, my abuelo cut one open with his pocketknife and asked me to try it. It was so bitter that, forty-five years later, my tongue flexes, and my mouth waters just thinking of it. If witches had poison apples, I had found El Cuco's poison orange.

Maybe that's why I didn't try it again until my mid-forties. It was the first year of the pandemic, and I was trying to recreate the ricotta and jam toast I ordered weekly from Sqirl, one of my favorite restaurants in LA. Unfortunately, a shopper subbed the orange marmalade I had requested with one made from bitter orange.

I dipped my finger into the jar and was pleasantly surprised when the punchy acidity hit my mouth. The sugar in the marmalade had taken the edge off, and the bitterness was no longer the most pronounced note. It paired beautifully with the creamy ricotta on my toast. It turns out all bitter orange needs to go from curmudgeon to happy camper is a little company. *Bendito*. (Bless your heart.)

SERVES 4

- 2 tablespoons salted butter, at room temperature
- 4 thick slices crusty artisan bread
- 1 cup full-fat ricotta cheese
- 2 tablespoons heavy cream
- ⅛ teaspoon kosher salt
- 4 tablespoons bitter orange jam (Seville oranges), warmed
- 1 tablespoon fresh whole tarragon leaves, for garnish
- Flaky salt, for garnish
- Zest of 1 orange

1. Preheat the oven to 450°F.
2. Line a baking sheet with parchment paper. Spread a quarter of the butter on one side of each slice of bread. Place the slices on the prepared baking sheet, buttered sides up. Toast them in the oven for 2 or 3 minutes then turn them over and toast for 2 or 3 minutes more, until lightly browned.
3. Meanwhile, in a mixing bowl, whisk together the ricotta, heavy cream, and salt by hand, or use a handheld electric mixer, until light and fluffy.
4. Arrange the toasted bread slices on a platter, butter-side up. Spoon equal amounts of the whipped ricotta on top of each one. Drizzle with the warm jam and top with the tarragon and a pinch of flaky salt and orange zest.

DULCE DE PAPAYA GRANOLA

Dulce de papaya, Spanish for candied papaya, is a very popular dessert in Puerto Rico. Strips of raw, young papaya are boiled in a spiced syrup until tender. In the process, they magically change color from a pale milky peach to a translucent pinkish-orange. Candied papaya is typically served with slices of farmer's cheese and a big cup of coffee. I adore it mixed into crunchy granola and layered into a parfait with fresh fruit or as a topping on Coconut Milk Breakfast Pudding (page 73). Note: I infuse habañero into this Dulce de Papaya Granola to add a soft note of smoky heat. But if you don't like any sort of heat, feel free to leave it out.

SERVES 10
(½ CUP SERVINGS)

Cooking oil spray

¾ cup coconut oil

1 habañero chile pepper (optional)

1 (17-ounce) can dulce de papaya (candied papaya in heavy syrup)

1 teaspoon kosher salt

1 teaspoon ground cinnamon

5 cups old-fashioned rolled oats

About 1 cup unsweetened flaked coconut (not shredded)

1 cup slivered raw almonds

1. Place a rack in the center of the oven and one directly underneath it, then preheat the oven to 350°F. Line a baking sheet with parchment paper and grease it with cooking oil spray. Set aside.

2. Warm the coconut oil in the microwave for about 30 seconds. (If not using the habañero, skip the next two steps.)

3. If you're using the habañero, smash it with the flat side of a chef's knife, then add it to the coconut oil and let it steep for 20 minutes.

4. Place a fine-mesh strainer over a bowl and pour the chile-infused oil through. Discard the solids.

5. Transfer the coconut oil to a bowl.

6. Place a fine-mesh strainer over a measuring cup, and collect ½ cup of the syrup from the can of dulce de papaya. Set aside and continue to drain the papaya so it dries out a bit. Refrigerate the remaining syrup in an airtight container and store it for future use.

7. Pour the reserved syrup into the bowl with the coconut oil, and stir in the salt and cinnamon.

8. Spread the mixture on one of the lined baking sheets in a single layer, then use the bottom of a measuring cup to compact it. Bake for 10 minutes (center rack), until fragrant and barely browned.

9. Meanwhile, cut the drained, candied papaya into ½-inch strips then coarsely chop them. Spread them on the other lined baking sheet and transfer to the lower rack, to bake along with the oat mixture.

10. After the granola has baked for 10 minutes, reduce the oven temperature to 300°F. Transfer the oat mixture baking sheet to a wire cooling rack and gently stir, without breaking up all of the clumps. Return the baking sheet to the oven's center rack and bake for 10 minutes more. The oats, almonds, and coconut should be toasted. The green papaya less tacky to the touch.

11. Transfer the oat-mixture baking sheet back to the wire rack. Scatter the bits of candied papaya over the surface and stir gently to distribute. Cool completely, then transfer to an airtight container, and store at room temperature for up to 2 weeks or freeze for up to 3 months.

COCONUT MILK BREAKFAST PUDDING

Many Puerto Ricans who come to the big continent live beneath the poverty line for a time, as they try to figure out a brand-new life in a brand-new world. My mother, twin brother, and I were no different; that often meant empty cupboards. We couldn't afford the fancy name-brand cereals that took up commercial space during our Saturday morning cartoons, but what we did have was Maizena cornstarch. My mother would use water with a splash of milk to make a breakfast pudding that she would dust with cinnamon, and to us, it was a mouth-watering amazing meal. We had no idea it was "poor people's" food. This recipe is based on that same pudding but made with all of the things that I'm sure my mother wished she could afford to make it with. Add texture with Dulce de Papaya Granola (page 70).

SERVES 4

- 4 cups coconut milk, well shaken
- ⅓ cup granulated sugar
- 2 (3-inch) cinnamon sticks
- 1 whole star anise
- 1 vanilla bean, split lengthwise (see Tip)
- Pinch of kosher salt
- 1 cup heavy whipping cream
- ⅓ cup cornstarch
- ¼ cup frozen/defrosted passion fruit pulp, for serving
- ¼ cup fresh blackberries, for serving
- Shaved coconut, for serving
- Mint leaves, for serving

1. In a heavy saucepan, combine the coconut milk, sugar, cinnamon sticks, star anise, vanilla bean, and the pinch of salt over medium heat. Cook, stirring, until the sugar has dissolved and the mixture starts to steam, then remove from the heat.
2. Take out the vanilla bean and using a knife, scrape its seeds into the steeped liquid, then return the bean to the pot. Let the mixture steep for 20 minutes.
3. Strain the coconut milk mixture through a fine-mesh strainer into a clean bowl (reserving the solids), then quickly return the liquid to the pot, and bring it to temperature over medium heat so it steams once again.
4. Meanwhile, add the heavy cream to a small bowl. Little by little, mix in the cornstarch, stirring until no lumps remain.
5. Using a whisk, gradually add the cornstarch mixture into the pot; keep whisking while the mixture comes to a boil. Cook for about 5 minutes more, or until it becomes glossy and smooth, with the consistency of thick cake batter.
6. Divide the coconut milk pudding evenly among 4 serving bowls. You can eat this breakfast pudding warm or cold; if you choose to go the cold route, cover each bowl with plastic wrap directly on the surface and transfer to the refrigerator to chill and set for at least 4 hours and up to 3 days.
7. To serve, top each portion with some of the passion fruit pulp and a blackberry or two. Finish with a sprinkle of shaved coconut and mint leaves.

TIP: **Reserve the scraped vanilla bean, anise pod, and cinnamon sticks. Dry and then mix them into a cup of sugar. Store it in an airtight container at room temperature. The aromatics will infuse the sugar with their flavor. The sugar is fantastic in baked goods and mixed into oatmeal or coffee.**

SORULLO WAFFLES
WITH PIQUE HONEY

Waffles were a mystery to me when I first encountered them laying sloppily on a tray at an all-you can-eat buffet in Reno, Nevada. My twin brother and I were eight years old and living with our father for the first time in our lives. While he wasn't much of a cook, the man loved a casino buffet almost as much as he loved drinking Carlo Rossi burgundy out of a gallon jug, and that is to say, a whole heck of a lot. My father loaded a plate with a giant Belgian waffle and absolutely drowned it in ladles of warm syrup. I was mesmerized by the way that golden liquid gathered in the perfectly square hollows of that waffle. Thus began my lifelong obsession.

These sorullo waffles are heavier than their traditional counterparts thanks to the cheesy cornmeal dough they're made with. I love their buttery, pillowy texture. But it's the deep amber crispy crevices created by the final sprinkle of cheddar cheese that I go crazy for. I serve them with pique honey, but if you want to get real Puerto Rican with it, serve them with a side of Spicy Mayo-Ketchup (page 42) as well.

You can prep and portion the dough up to a few days ahead of time. Flatten the balls of dough into discs the size of your waffle maker and store in the fridge for up to three days. Just make sure to separate the layers with parchment or wax paper. You can also freeze them for up to three months.

MAKES 4 WAFFLES

- A double recipe Sorullos dough (see page 77)
- Cooking oil spray
- ¼ cup shredded cheddar cheese
- ¼ cup honey (use a plant-based alternative for a vegan preparation)
- 2 tablespoons Pique (page 41)

1. Preheat your oven to the lowest temperature in preparation for keeping the waffles warm. Make the Sorullo dough. While the cornmeal dough cools to a pliable consistency, preheat a waffle iron.

2. Pinch off a chunk of the dough, about the size of a tennis ball, and roll it into a smooth sphere using your palms. Press it into a flat disc that's about ½ inch thick and the same circumference as your waffle maker.

3. Grease your waffle iron with cooking oil spray and heat according to the manufacturer's directions. Place the disc of dough in the center of the iron and press down slowly until the iron has shut. Cook the sorullo waffle for 5 to 7 minutes, until lightly golden and crisped. They will sizzle at the start and become quiet as they approach doneness.

4. Open the waffle maker and sprinkle the entire surface of the waffle with 1 tablespoon of cheddar cheese. Close the waffle maker, and continue cooking the waffle until the cheese turns crispy and amber, about 2 minutes. Keep the waffles warm in the oven until they're all done, and regrease the waffle iron each time you make a new waffle.

5. Meanwhile, in a small bowl, stir together the honey and Pique until well blended. Drizzle over the warm waffles and serve.

SORULLOS

MAKES 16 SORULLOS

- 1 cup plus 2 tablespoons water
- 1 teaspoon fine sea salt
- ¾ cup medium-grind cornmeal
- ¼ cup grated Edam cheese
- Corn oil for frying

Sorullos are thunderously crisp Puerto Rican cornmeal fritters that get their name from their stubby, hand-rolled, cigar shape. They are deep fried, giving them a textured, crunchy outer shell and a luscious, velvety inside.

This recipe couldn't be simpler or more adaptable. There are multiple ways to change it up: You can add a touch of sugar and vanilla for sweet sorullos or substitute the water with coconut milk for a creamier result. You can also substitute the Edam cheese with Gouda, Gruyère, or cheddar. Use a plant-based cheese that melts well for a vegan preparation.

You can prep the dough and shape the sorullos ahead of time and refrigerate them in an airtight container for a few days. If you're layering them on top of each other, separate the layers with parchment or wax paper. You can also freeze the sorullos on a baking sheet until firm, then seal them in an airtight container and freeze them for up to three months. Serve sorullos with Mayo-Ketchup (page 42) as a dipping sauce. Use this dough to make my Sorullo Waffles with Pique Honey (page 74).

1. In a heavy pot , bring the water and the salt to a boil over high heat. Reduce the heat to medium, then add the cornmeal, using a whisk to quickly bring together a cohesive dough (like a polenta) that pulls away from the sides of the pot; this should take only a couple of minutes. Remove from the heat.

2. Gently fold in the cheese until melted and evenly combined , then transfer the dough to a cutting board.

3. When the cornmeal dough cools to a pliable consistency, pinch off a chunk that's about the size of a golf ball. Roll the ball into a cigar shape using the palms of your hands. Repeat with the remainder of the dough.

4. Line a plate with paper towels. Add 2 inches of frying oil to a skillet. Heat to 365°F. Fry the sorullos in batches, 3 to 4 minutes total, until they deepen in color and develop a crispy outer layer. Drain on the paper towel-lined plate and serve.

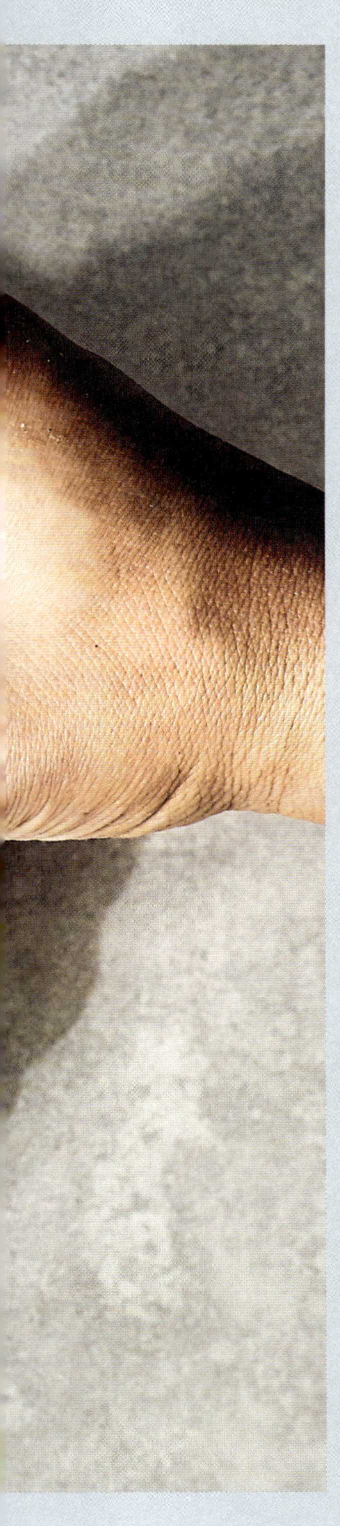

Things to Eat with Your Hands

Empanadillas, Sandwiches, and Wraps

AREPAS DE COCO

Puerto Rican arepas de coco are different than other arepas in Latin cuisine, as they are made with flour and coconut milk instead of cornmeal and water. They are a fry bread of sorts, easy to put together and best eaten while still steaming hot. My Abuela Dora served them with a pat of margarine and a cup of milky coffee. But you can use them like a pita bread of sorts, and stuff them with whatever you desire. Use them to make my Stuffed BLT Arepas de Coco (page 82).

MAKES 8 AREPAS

- 1 cup all-purpose flour, plus more for dusting
- ½ teaspoon baking powder
- 2 tablespoons granulated sugar
- ⅛ teaspoon kosher salt
- ½ cup coconut milk, well shaken
- Canola oil (or other neutral cooking oil), for greasing and frying

1. Generously dust a work surface with flour. In a mixing bowl, whisk together the flour, baking powder, sugar, and salt. Add the coconut milk and stir with a fork just until it gathers to form a dough that's sticky but not wet. Transfer the dough to the work surface, then wipe the bowl clean and lightly grease it.

2. Knead the dough for about 5 minutes, or until it becomes smooth, stretchy, and no longer sticky. If the dough is too wet, add a little more flour, 1 tablespoon at a time. If it is too dry, add a little water, 1 tablespoon at a time. Return the dough to the bowl, cover with a damp kitchen towel, and let the dough rest in a warm spot for 30 minutes. (It will not rise.)

3. Divide the rested dough into 2 equal portions. Dust a work surface with flour and roll each portion out until ¼ inch thick, about the thickness of an ear lobe. Use a 4-inch biscuit cutter (or the lid of a wide mouth mason jar) to cut out 8 rounds total.

4. Set a large skillet or cast-iron pan over medium heat. Pour in about an inch of oil. Once the oil has reached 365°F (or a bit of the dough bubbles as soon as it hits the oil), add the arepas in 2 batches and cook for 2 to 3 minutes on each side, until they are puffed, crisped on the outside, and cooked through.

STUFFED BLT AREPAS DE COCO

During my adolescence, my mother wouldn't allow me to sleepover at the houses of "*Americanos*," reinforcing the unspoken belief that though we lived in Texas and were US citizens, we were not to think of ourselves as American. Her stance softened only once. I was ten the first time I attended a sleepover at Angelique's, who lived a few doors down in our suburban neighborhood. I was shocked my mother allowed it, as Angelique and her mother were both blondes with startingly blue eyes—a combination my mother was convinced belonged only to racist witches. (It makes me giggle that her first grandchild, my son, is blonde with blue eyes.)

It was strange being in the belly of the beast. Angelique's house did not smell of sofrito, but it did smell of bacon. We had BLTs for dinner, and Angelique needed help picking her jaw up off the floor when I asked what a BLT was. She exclaimed that it was the best sandwich ever, but a few bites in, I felt sorry for her. The mushy white bread stuck to the roof of my mouth. Her mother had really gone light on the bacon, and the only thing I could taste was the mayo and watery lettuce and tomato. I know it sounds silly to count eating a BLT as trauma, but it was the first time I realized how *other* I was. I consider this mashup recipe a moment of healing.

If you're running short on time, you can find frozen arepas de coco at well-stocked Latin markets. If you want to dig deep, try making a half batch of my Arepas de Coco (page 81). You can make this recipe vegan by substituting the bacon and mayo for plant-based versions.

SERVES 4

- Half batch Arepas de Coco dough (see page 81) or 4 store-bought frozen/thawed, arepas de coco
- 8 slices thick-cut bacon
- 2 teaspoons red wine vinegar
- 1 tablespoon plus 1½ teaspoons extra-virgin olive oil
- ½ teaspoon garlic salt
- ⅛ teaspoon freshly ground black pepper
- 4 slices beefsteak tomato, cut ¼ inch thick
- 1 small ripe avocado
- 1 lime, cut in half
- Corn oil, for frying
- ¼ cup full-fat or low-fat mayonnaise
- 8 large leaves butter lettuce, for serving

1. Make a half recipe of Arepas de Coco dough, and rest it for 30 minutes. (If using store-bought arepas, skip to next step.)
2. Preheat the oven to 450°F.
3. Line a rimmed baking sheet with aluminum foil and set an ovenproof wire rack inside it. Lay the strips of bacon on the wire rack, and roast for 15 to 17 minutes, until crisped. Cool, then cut each slice crosswise in half. Set aside.
4. In a small bowl, whisk together the vinegar, olive oil, garlic salt, and pepper to form a well-blended dressing. Arrange the tomato slices on a large plate and drizzle with the dressing.
5. Remove the seed from the avocado. Use a large soup spoon to scoop the flesh from each half in one piece. Slice the halves crosswise into ¼-inch-thick pieces. Place them on a small plate and squeeze lime juice over the slices to prevent browning. Set aside.

6. Line a plate with paper towels. Set a large skillet or cast-iron pan over medium heat. Drizzle in about an inch of corn oil. Once the oil has reached 365°F (or a bit of the dough bubbles as soon as it hits the oil), add the arepas and cook for 2 to 3 minutes on each side, until they are puffed, crisped on the outside, and cooked through. Take the arepas out of the oil and cool them on the prepared plate for 1 minute.

7. Cut a 3-inch-long slit into the side edge of one arepa and spread open to create a pocket. Spread 1 tablespoon of mayo inside the still warm arepa. Add 2 leaves of butter lettuce, a tomato slice, a quarter of the avocado slices, and a quarter of the crisped bacon. Repeat to create the remaining stuffed BLT arepas. Serve hot.

TRIPLETA BURGERS

The *tripleta* is a beloved sandwich on the island—a mix of grilled beef, ham, and roasted pork, that's topped with a smattering of lettuce and tomato and finished with a final layer of shoestring fries or potato sticks. It's a symphony of texture and umami. This is all of the goodness of a tripleta mashed with one of the most iconic sandwiches in American history. Is it a little too too? ABSOLUTELY. And it is worth it.

SERVES 4

- 1 tablespoon corn oil
- ½ pound ground beef, preferably boneless short rib
- ½ pound ground pork
- 1 teaspoon Sazón (page 33)
- 1 teaspoon kosher salt
- 8 slices Swiss cheese
- 8 slices Black Forest ham
- 4 Martin's Potato Rolls, or your favorite hamburger buns
- 4 tablespoons (½ stick) salted butter, melted
- 4 tablespoons Spicy Mayo-Ketchup (page 42)
- ½ (packed) cup shredded iceberg lettuce
- 4 slices beefsteak tomato
- 1 cup shoestring potato sticks

1. In a cast-iron grill pan, heat the oil on the stovetop or outdoor grill over medium-high heat.
2. In a mixing bowl, season the ground beef and pork with the Sazón. Divide the mixture into 4 portions of equal size, then loosely shape into patties. Season them with the salt.
3. Add them to the hot grill pan and cook to your desired degree of doneness, turning them over every few minutes.
4. After their final flip, layer two slices of the cheese atop each burger. Cook until just melted, then transfer the burgers to a cutting board to rest.
5. Add the ham slices to the grill pan and cook just until their edges are crisp and turn a light golden brown. Transfer to the cutting board.
6. Brush the cut sides of the rolls with the butter and place them face down on the grill pan until toasted.
7. When ready to assemble the burgers, spread about ½ tablespoon of mayo-ketchup on each bottom bun. Top with the lettuce and a slice of tomato. Add the cheese-topped burger patty, two slices of ham, and top with a quarter cup of potato sticks. Spread the top buns with the remaining mayo ketchup, place on the burgers, and serve.

COCONUT SHRIMP & GREEN MANGO SLAW WRAPS

I've never been a patient person, especially as a kid. So waiting for the bounty of mangoes on our tree in Mayaguez to ripen made me grit my teeth. I took the green ones, their flesh the lightest yellow, sliced them, soaked them in salty water, and ate them just like that—tart, briny, and crisp. Almost always, the liquid dripped off the slices and soaked the front of my T-shirt. My abuela threw pleas at me like fastballs, *"¡No seas animal!"* ("Don't be an animal!")

If you've never had a green mango, it is a textural delight. I love it shredded and paired with fresh herbs in a slaw, dressed with lime juice and red pepper flakes. It's even better in this wrap with juicy, crispy coconut shrimp. If you're short on time, skip battering and frying the shrimp with shredded coconut and panko and use pre-cooked cocktail shrimp instead. Sprinkle in toasted shredded coconut to taste. If you're vegetarian, sub the fish sauce with half a teaspoon of white miso and use plant-based shrimp.

SERVES 4

Slaw

2 firm, unripe green mangoes, peeled, pitted, and shredded (sub with green apples or jicama)

1 (packed) cup shredded green cabbage

½ cup coarsely chopped cilantro (leaves and tender stems)

½ cup coarsely chopped fresh mint leaves

3 scallions, thinly sliced (white and green parts)

Kosher salt

1 teaspoon fish sauce

2 tablespoons fresh lime juice

2 teaspoons light brown sugar

¼ teaspoon crushed red pepper flakes

Filling

1 pound large shrimp, shelled and deveined (21–30 or 16–20 count; no tails)

1 teaspoon kosher salt

½ cup rice flour

1 teaspoon Adobo (page 30)

2 large eggs

¾ (packed) cup shredded unsweetened coconut

½ cup plain panko breadcrumbs

¼ cup sesame seeds

Oil, for frying (use canola, corn, vegetable, or avocado oil)

4 (12-inch) flour tortillas, for serving

1. Make the slaw: In a mixing bowl, toss together the mango, cabbage, cilantro, mint, and scallions. Sprinkle with ½ teaspoon salt, toss, and transfer the slaw to a colander. Set the colander in the empty mixing bowl for a minimum of 30 minutes and up to 8 hours. The salt breaks down the shredded cabbage, expelling excess water, and creating a crunchier and more flavorful slaw.

2. When you're ready to assemble the wraps, take the cabbage mixture out of the colander and place it on a strip of paper towels. Top it with a second strip of paper towels. Roll it up and squeeze to remove excess moisture. Empty the mixing bowl the colander was in. Return the slaw to the mixing bowl.

3. In a liquid measuring cup, combine the fish sauce, lime juice, brown sugar, red pepper flakes, and ⅛ teaspoon salt, stirring until the sugar dissolves, then drizzle that mixture over the slaw and toss to coat evenly. Refrigerate while you make the filling.

4. Make the filling: Set the shrimp in a large mixing bowl and sprinkle with the salt. Mix thoroughly. Set up 3 medium bowls. Combine the flour and ¾ teaspoon of the Adobo in the first one. Lightly beat the eggs in the second bowl. Combine the remaining ¼ teaspoon of Adobo, the coconut, panko, and sesame seeds in the third.

Continues

5. Working with a few shrimp at a time, dip them into the seasoned flour, then the eggs, and finally into the coconut mixture until completely coated, shaking off any excess. Place the coated shrimp on a plate.

6. In a deep, heavy skillet, pour in oil to a depth of 2 inches over medium-high heat. Line a plate with paper towels. Once the oil registers 365°F on an instant-read thermometer, add a third of the shrimp. Fry for 2 minutes, or until a light golden brown, then use tongs to turn them over and fry for 2 minutes more. Transfer the coconut-fried shrimp to the paper towel-lined plate. Repeat with the remaining shrimp.

7. Transfer the shrimp to a cutting board and coarsely chop them. Warm a tortilla over a burner or in a large pan or griddle just until it's pliable, then place it on a cutting board.

8. Place a quarter of the slaw in the lower third of the warm tortilla. Top with a quarter of the chopped coconut shrimp. Fold the bottom edge of the tortilla over the filling, and then use your index finger to push the filling toward you to tighten up the roll. Fold the left and right sides of the tortilla toward the center, then finish rolling up the tortilla to form a wrap. Repeat with the remaining tortillas and filling. Cut each wrap through the center and serve.

PEANUT BUTTER, BACON, & CANDIED PLANTAIN SAMMIES

This is the Spanglish version of Elvis's famous peanut butter, bacon, and banana sandwich. And while I didn't grow up with Elvis's music, I did grow up with Ricky Martin's. If Ricky had a peanut butter and bacon sandwich, he would undoubtedly top it with buttery, caramelized sweet plantain instead of bananas. (I have not run this by Ricky, but it seems like a perfectly reasonable fantasy.) This open-faced sandwich is made on thick artisan bread, like slices of ciabatta or boule, and finished with a touch of lime zest. The recipe can easily be made vegetarian by substituting the bacon and butter with plant-based options.

SERVES 4

- 4 slices thick-cut bacon
- 8 tablespoons (1 stick) salted butter
- 8 frozen/defrosted ripe plantain slices, cut into ¼-inch-thick rounds
- ¼ (packed) cup dark brown sugar
- 1 (3-inch) cinnamon stick
- 1 whole star anise
- 4 thick slices crusty artisan bread
- ¾ cup crunchy peanut butter
- Lime zest, for serving

1. Preheat the oven to 400°F.

2. Line a rimmed baking sheet with aluminum foil and set an ovenproof wire rack inside. Lay the strips of bacon on the wire rack and roast for about 20 minutes, or until crisp. Transfer to paper towels to drain. Once the bacon has cooled, coarsely chop it into ¼-inch pieces.

3. Meanwhile, in a sauté pan, melt 4 tablespoons of the butter over medium heat. Add the plantains and cook for 4 or 5 minutes, stirring occasionally, until their edges caramelize.

4. Reduce the heat to medium-low and add the sugar. Cook until it has dissolved, then gently stir in ¼ cup water, being careful not to break up the plantains. Add the cinnamon stick and star anise. Cook for about 10 minutes, or until the pan liquid becomes syrupy enough to coat and caramelize the plantains.

5. In a large skillet, melt 2 tablespoons of butter over medium heat. Add the bread slices and cook just until lightly toasted. Add the remaining 2 tablespoons of butter to the pan; once that has melted, turn over the slices to toast them on the second side. Transfer the toasted bread to a paper towel-lined plate.

6. Remove the cinnamon stick and star anise pod from the plantain liquid; pat dry and reserve them. Remove the plantain from the liquid and reserve the liquid (see Tip).

7. Spread about 3 tablespoons of peanut butter on each slice of bread. Layer a quarter of the candied plantains on top of each slice.

8. Scatter the crisped bacon evenly over the plantains. Drizzle a bit of the reserved plantain pan syrup over the bacon, and scatter the lime zest evenly over the top. Cut each slice in half on the diagonal and serve.

TIP: Any leftover plantain liquid can be used to sweeten yogurt or oatmeal. Add the dried reserved cinnamon and star anise pod to a cup of sugar to flavor it. Store in an airtight container.

MORCILLA SLOPPY JOES

My mother was the first person to give me a taste of *morcilla* (blood sausage). The charcoal-black sausage had white bits of rice in it, and I imagined it as the inspiration for the cover of my new kindergarten Mead composition notebook. It had been fried, so the skin had a snap to it that gave way to an unctuous and crumbly filling. My mother had skewered slices of morcilla with toothpicks and placed them on a platter at a family gathering. By the collection of toothpicks next to my plate, it was obvious that I was the only one going hard. It tickled her how much I loved it. I had no idea it was blood sausage.

Blood sausage is my favorite sausage of all time, and it is truly fantastic. If you've never had it, I urge you to try it and tell me differently. (If you try it and hate it, lie to me.) This Spanglish Sloppy Joe mash-up is one of my favorite ways to eat it. Puerto Rican–style morcilla is a black sausage made up of pork blood, sofrito, and rice. It's tough to source stateside, but worth the effort. Mexican-style morcilla (moronga) is more widely available. It's typically rice-free and mixed with offal, so the color can run lighter. Both versions work in this recipe.

SERVES 6

- 2 tablespoons Annatto Oil (page 37)
- 1 cup Recaíto (page 34)
- 2 tablespoons tomato paste
- 1½ pounds morcilla, casings removed, cut into ¼-inch dice
- 1 cup ketchup
- 2 teaspoons Sazón (page 33)
- 1 teaspoon powdered mustard
- ½ teaspoon crushed red pepper flakes
- Kosher salt and freshly ground black pepper
- 2 tablespoons salted butter, melted
- 6 hamburger buns, for serving

1. Heat the Annatto Oil in a large, heavy, nonstick sauté pan over medium heat until it shimmers. Stir in the Recaíto and tomato paste. Cook for about 2 minutes, or until thickened. Add the morcilla and cook for 5 minutes, using a sturdy spoon to break it up as it browns.

2. Stir in the ketchup, 1 cup water, the Sazón, powdered mustard, and red pepper flakes. Reduce the heat to low, partially cover, and cook for 20 minutes, stirring occasionally. The mixture will darken in color and thicken considerably. Season with salt and black pepper to taste. The yield is about 5 cups.

3. Brush the butter on the cut sides of the buns; toast cut sides down on a griddle or in a toaster oven until lightly browned. Place the bottom buns, toasted sides up, on individual plates. Spoon equal portions of the morcilla on the buns, complete with the top buns, and serve.

CHEESESTEAK EMPANADILLAS

My Abuela Dora made *empanadillas* (turnovers) by the dozens, like she was preparing to feed the neighborhood. She cooked up big batches of *picadillo* (ground beef cooked in a tomato sauce), stuffing it into premade discs of dough that she would have me seal with a fork. Then she would wrap the empanadillas in wax paper and stuff them into freezer bags. She stocked our freezer until it spit out a bag of empanadillas every time you opened it. If you opened that freezer and no empanadillas hit you, it was time to make more.

Finely dicing the classic Philly cheesesteak ingredients in this recipe gives the filling the texture of traditional Puerto Rican picadillo. Bonus: the cheese tucks into all of the nooks and crannies. You can find the premade discs of dough in the freezer aisle of most Latino grocers. But it's simple enough to make your own dough, and make the rounds a little thicker, so they really hold up to the cheese and steak filling. Uncooked empanadillas can be wrapped in wax paper and refrigerated in an airtight container for up to five days or frozen until firm, then placed into a zip-top bag, sealed, and frozen for up to two months.

SERVES 8

- 1 recipe Empanadilla Dough (page 95) or 8 (6-inch) store-bought empanadilla wrappers
- 3 tablespoons canola oil, plus more for frying
- 1 large white onion, cut into a small dice
- 1 red bell pepper, stemmed, seeded, and cut into a small dice
- 1 green bell pepper, stemmed, seeded, and cut into a small dice
- 1 teaspoon kosher salt, divided
- 1 tablespoon distilled white vinegar
- 12 ounces finely-sliced rib eye steak (see Tip)
- ¼ teaspoon freshly ground black pepper
- ½ pound (8 round slices) provolone cheese

1. If you're making the Empanadilla Dough, stack the 8 rounds, separating them each with wax paper. Cover with a clean tea towel and refrigerate while you make the filling.

2. In a large heavy skillet, heat 2 tablespoons of the oil over medium heat. Once it shimmers, stir in the onion and red and green bell peppers. Sprinkle with ¼ teaspoon of the salt and cook for about 10 minutes, stirring occasionally, or until the peppers soften considerably and the onion begins to brown. Transfer to a bowl and stir in the vinegar.

3. Give the rib eye a few rough chops and season with the remaining salt and the black pepper.

4. Return the skillet to the stovetop over medium-high heat. Add the remaining tablespoon of oil. Add the first batch of meat and cook it just until no trace of red remains. Transfer the first batch to the bowl of cooked onion and peppers. Cook the remaining batch the same way (without adding more oil), adding it to the bowl to cool.

5. When you're ready to assemble, place one empanadilla round on your work surface. Lay a slice of provolone, centered on each round of dough. Scoop an eighth of the filling (about 3 tablespoons) on the cheese on the bottom third of the empanadilla round. Fold over the

TIP: If you can't source finely sliced rib eye, purchase a boneless rib eye steak, place it in the freezer for 30 minutes or until it begins to harden, and slice it yourself. Alternatively, you can finely dice the steak about the same size as the onion and peppers.

Continues

dough in the shape of a half-moon, folding in and then crimping the edges of the empanadilla with the tines of a fork to seal it shut. Before the last crimp, press down lightly on the filled empanadilla to ensure there are no pockets of air. Refrigerate the empanadillas as you work and while the frying oil heats.

6. Pour at least 3 inches of oil into a large heavy pot. Place over medium heat until the oil registers 350°F on an instant-read thermometer. Prepare a wire cooling rack with paper towels underneath, or line a large platter with several layers of paper towels.

7. Fry 3 to 4 empanadillas at a time, for about 8 minutes, or until crisped and golden brown all over and the cheese has melted inside, turning them carefully as needed. Transfer to the wire rack briefly to drain. Serve warm.

EMPANADILLA DOUGH

MAKES 8 ROUNDS

- 2 cups all-purpose flour, plus more as needed and for dusting
- ¼ teaspoon baking powder
- 1½ teaspoons kosher salt
- 2 tablespoons vegetable shortening, frozen until firm
- 2 tablespoon salted butter, frozen until firm
- 1 large egg, lightly beaten
- ½ cup ice-cold water, plus more as needed

Empanadillas are a beloved staple in Puerto Rican cuisine, a quintessential part of our street food culture, and my Abuela Dora's favorite thing to make. These turnovers can be filled with anything from classic beef *picadillo* (ground beef cooked in sofrito-based tomato sauce) to plain cheese. They are most often fried, though they can be baked. Depending on where you're from on the island, how they're shaped, and what they're filled with, they can also be called *empanadas*, *pastelitos*, or *pastelillos*. People will argue endlessly about which name is right. I just call them delicious.

My abuela bought her empanadilla dough premade, rolled out in perfect circles that were stacked tall and separated by wax paper. It is definitely a time-saver, but my local grocery store doesn't carry empanadilla dough. So I learned how to make it. You can freeze this dough for up to three months. Just make sure you wrap it well.

1. In a mixing bowl, combine the flour, baking powder, and salt. Using the large-hole side of a box grater, grate the shortening and the butter directly into the bowl. Using a fork, toss until they are completely coated with flour.

2. Make a well in the center of the flour mixture. Add the egg and 2 tablespoons of the ice-cold water, then stir with a fork to begin incorporating. Continue to add the cold water in 2-tablespoons increments until the mixture starts to clump together and form a dough. If you add too much water and the dough becomes sticky, add a little more flour.

3. Lightly flour a work surface. Transfer the dough there and form it into a ball, kneading it with the palm of your hand for 5 to 6 minutes, until smooth and elastic. When you stretch the dough over itself, it should not tear. Wrap the dough in plastic wrap and refrigerate for at least 30 minutes and up to 24 hours.

4. When you're ready to make the empanadilla, prep your work surface with two pieces of parchment paper. Divide the dough into four equal portions and place a damp tea towel over them.

5. Working with one portion at a time, roll the dough into a ball, then divide that ball into two equal pieces. Roll each one of those into a ball, place it in between the two pieces of parchment, then use a rolling pin to roll them into a total of 8 rounds about 8 inches in diameter—but not so thin that you can see through the dough.

PLANTAIN CHIP–BREADED CHICKEN NUGGETS

I can eat these crispy golden nuggets of goodness until I hate myself. Pair them with Sorullo Waffles with Pique Honey (page 74) for pure Spanglish perfection! If you're vegetarian, substitute the chicken with a plant-based option. If you don't eat eggs, you can substitute them with a slurry of ¼ cup cornstarch and 3 to 4 tablespoons water, mixed until a pasty batter forms.

SERVES 4

- Vegetable oil, for frying
- 2 tablespoons cornstarch
- 2 tablespoons rice flour
- 1 teaspoon Sazón (page 33)
- 2 teaspoons Adobo (page 30)
- ½ teaspoon kosher salt
- 2 large eggs, lightly beaten
- ⅓ cup plain seltzer water
- 8 ounces plain plantain chips, finely crushed (a generous 2½ cups)
- 4 boneless, skinless chicken thighs (about 1 pound total)
- Spicy Mayo-Ketchup (page 42), for dipping

1. Preheat the oven to 200°F.
2. In a Dutch oven, pour in oil to a depth of 2 inches over medium heat.
3. Meanwhile, in a mixing bowl, stir together the cornstarch, rice flour, Sazón, Adobo, and salt. Add the eggs, then pour in the seltzer, stirring with a sturdy spoon to form a thin batter. Place the crushed plantain chips in a shallow bowl.
4. Chop the chicken thighs into approximately 2-inch pieces. Trimming any excess fat.
5. Once the oil registers 365°F on an instant-read thermometer, coat the chicken tenders in the batter, shake off any excess, then lay them in the crushed chips, making sure they are completely coated. Repeat the process to create a thick covering. Carefully add to the hot oil, laying them in the pan away from you, and fry for 4 to 5 minutes, turning them over, until golden, crisped, and cooked through (internal temperature 160°F). Serve with Spicy Mayo-Ketchup (page 42).

Part Two

A Puerto
Gets Tor

Rican
n in Two

I was six when *Mami* shook me gently in the dark. "*Levántate*," ("Get up,") she whispered, her voice thick with something I didn't understand yet. My twin brother and I sat up, bleary-eyed and got ready for our first plane ride. I didn't realize that we were leaving our homeland of Puerto Rico for good. I boarded the plane without looking back, as if we were running late for school. I chewed the gum my mother gave me and stared jealously at the American Airlines pin she had fastened onto my brother's shirt while she wiped the occasional tear from her face.

When I stepped out of the plane onto the metal staircase, I breathed in cold air for the first time. Inhaling hurt my lungs, but I was fascinated with the big bursts of white smoke that escaped my mouth with every exhale. Had I become a dragon? Is that what happens when you fly?

The wonder that fueled those first steps didn't last.

We had traded the sultry heat of San Juan for the gray chill of a Texas winter. This new world was exciting at first, but after a few weeks, I started to feel like I was living outside of my skin. There was no mention of my culture. Ever. I had to soak it up in snippets, surviving off whatever scraps I could find: The occasional whiff of pork frying. The faraway lilt of a fast-paced merengue. Someone next to us in traffic, with the Puerto Rican flag dangling from their rearview mirror. The love for my island so intense my heart would surge at the mere sight of it.

Everything about the city was gray and cold: the buildings, the people, the wind whipping through the streets, propelling gas fumes through naked trees. I missed the saturated colors of my island, the blossoms of a *flamboyán* tree ablaze during a sunset, the concrete houses of old San Juan set closely together, painted in pastels of every shade like a parade of stone cupcakes. I longed for the headiness of hot salt air intermingled with the perfume of a tree heavy with ripe mangoes.

I missed being lulled to sleep by the song of the *coquí,* our native tree frog. In Houston, the wails of police cars keep me awake at night. In Puerto Rico, my brother and I put a conch shell to our ear to hear the ocean trapped inside. In Houston, we collect a shell casing and wonder when the bullets rung out and why.

At my new school, I stared at the alphabet above the chalkboard and recited the letters in my mind in Spanish. I wondered where the *CH, LL*, *Ñ,* and the *RR* had gone. My teacher was giving us a spelling test. She walked around the classroom, reciting words I could not understand. Everyone was scribbling on their paper but me. The kid behind me poked me with his pencil and pointed to his paper. "Spell it," he said. I looked at the word and copied it to my paper letter by letter: F. U. C. K.

He smiled. I smiled back—finally, a friend.

Mrs. White stopped at my table and looked at my paper. She snatched it off my desk and said: "What is this?" I thought I'd been caught cheating. But Mrs. White kept pointing at the word I had written. "What is this?!?!" she screamed.

I did not understand what was happening. I stared over at my new friend, whose shoulders shook from holding in the laughter.

I don't remember how she got my favorite Donkey Kong Junior pencil out of my hands and into hers. But at some point in her barrage of words I could not understand, Mrs. White became so overcome with emotion that she snapped my pencil in two. That was the last straw.

She might as well have split me down the middle. At that moment, all of the frustration from the move washed over me like a wave ripping apart a sandcastle. I wanted to go home, where I didn't have to work at being understood, where kids didn't make fun of foreign words that were slow to fall out of my mouth. Rage bubbled over me. It came out in a garbled cry as I stood and flipped my desk over.

I ran out of the room and straight into a maze of school hallways—I did not know where to go, just that I had to keep going. I inhaled deeply and followed the scent of beef simmering in the cafeteria.

Today was Sloppy Joe Day. I walked up to where the lunch lady stood over the hotel pan of ground beef in tomato sauce and stared.

"Can I help you?" The lunch lady looked over at me suspiciously. I stared blankly at her. She had brown skin like my mother. "*¿Qué quieres*?" she asked. ("What do you want?") My eyes widened as I realized she spoke Spanish! I stood as straight as I could.

"*Necesito un cuchillo*," ("I need a knife,") I said calmly.

She stared at me. "*¿Pa' qué?*" ("What for?")

"*Voy a matar a mi maestra.*" ("I am going to kill my teacher.")

She nodded, pursing her lips. "*Espérate.*" ("Hold on.")

She returned a minute later holding a little white plastic knife, the kind that comes in a plastic bag with a fork and a spoon and a salt and pepper packet. As a fifty-year-old woman now, I look back at that moment in awe at the absolute zero cares this lunch lady had left to give. As a seven-year-old, I felt I had made a comrade in arms.

I hid in a bathroom stall for almost an hour, gathering up the courage and the words I needed to knife my teacher. I ran through the classroom door screaming in my best English, "I keel you!" But as soon as the words were out of my mouth, I knew that the only person getting killed was me. Inside, my mother glowered at me, her black hair sticking out every which way from underneath a white knitted cap. The beating started in the school hallway, continued in the car, and ended in our apartment.

FUCK.

I realized that day I had to say goodbye to Puerto Rico. There was no way back home. I was one of the avocado seeds my mother speared with toothpicks and kept in jars of water on the kitchen counter. I would grow here, but I would never bloom. I would have to adapt.

This was our new life, and if I wanted to feel like I was back with my friends and family, I would have to make do with the bowl of sancocho my mother placed in front of me. The backs of my thighs were still raw, and I tried my best not to put weight on them. I stared at the welt on my arm as I dipped my spoon into the bowl.

Something about this Puerto Rican beef stew brought me right back to my Abuela Alicia's table in San Juan, back to everything I loved about my island. The steam that rose from the stew, scented with cilantro, caressed my face like an ocean breeze. Its broth, heavy with the starch of yuca, potato, plantain, and taro, a blanket for my insides. The first bite of *tripa*, its gelatinous beefiness spreading on my tongue, whispered, "*Vámonos.*" ("Let's go.")

Sancocho is a poor man's stew, and that day, it was also my mother's apology. This new world was going to take some getting used to.

Things to Warm You

Soups and Stews

OXTAIL SANCOCHO

Sancocho is pure comfort in a bowl. The beef in this Latin-American meat stew is fall-off-the-bone tender. The root vegetables thicken the hearty broth, making it almost velvety. Though this stew takes about three and a half hours of simmering, and has quite a few ingredients, it's well worth the time. In this case, the sum is much greater than its parts. To save time, you can use store-bought recaíto, adobo, and sazón. If you can't source any yuca or calabaza, just sub them with potatoes and sweet potatoes. You can substitute the oxtail with short ribs or chicken thighs. If you want to make this recipe vegan, swap the oxtails for more root vegetables and substitute the chicken broth with vegetable broth.

Refrigerate your leftover sancocho in an airtight container for a few days. If you want to freeze it, divide it into individual portions; it can keep for up to two months. To prevent freezer burn, fill the containers to the top and cover the surface of the stew with plastic wrap or wax paper.

You can reheat sancocho on the stove or in the microwave. You might want to add a bit of water to thin the broth. Make sure to heat the stew until the meat and vegetables are steaming.

SERVES 8

- 1 tablespoon olive oil
- 4 pounds oxtails, patted dry
- Kosher salt and freshly ground black pepper
- ½ cup Recaíto (page 34)
- 1 tablespoon Adobo (page 30)
- 1½ teaspoons Sazón (page 33)
- ½ teaspoon dried oregano
- 2 bay leaves
- 6 ounces tomato paste
- 14 cups chicken stock or broth, plus more as needed
- 2 cups dry red wine, such as Merlot, Tempranillo, or Cabernet
- 4 Yukon Gold potatoes, peeled and cut into a large dice
- 1 medium yuca, peeled and woody center removed, then cut into a large dice (may substitute with frozen yuca or tarot)
- 1 calabaza pumpkin, peeled, seeded, and cut into a large dice (may substitute with acorn squash or sweet potato)
- 2 green plantains, peeled, seeded, and cut into 2-inch thick rounds
- 2 ears fresh corn, husked, and cut crosswise into 1-inch rounds
- Cooked white rice, for serving (optional)
- Cilantro leaves, for garnish

1. In large heavy pot, heat the olive oil over medium-high heat until it shimmers. Season the oxtails generously with salt and pepper. Add the oxtails, in batches, and sear for a few minutes on all sides until nicely browned. Transfer them to a plate as you work.

2. Reduce the heat to medium. Drain/discard all but 2 tablespoons of rendered fat in the pot, then add the Recaíto and cook for about 2 minutes, or until fragrant.

3. Add the Adobo, Sazón, oregano, and bay leaves. Cook for 1 minute to bloom the spices. Add the tomato paste, using a wooden spoon to dislodge any browned bits in the pot.

4. Add the stock and the wine; once the liquids boil, reduce the heat to medium-low. Return all the oxtails to the pot, along with any of their resting juices. Partially cover and cook for about 3 hours. During that time, taste the stew once or twice and add salt and/or pepper as needed. Use a light touch, as the more the stock cooks down, the saltier it becomes.

5. Uncover; skim off/discard any fat that accumulates on the surface, then add the potatoes, yuca, pumpkin, plantains, and corn, stirring to distribute evenly. Add stock as needed to make sure the vegetables are covered. Partially cover and cook for about 30 minutes, or until the root vegetables are fork-tender. Taste again, and season as needed. Discard the bay leaves.

6. Serve the stew in large bowls with a side of rice, if using, and garnish with the cilantro.

FRICASÉ CHICKEN & DUMPLINGS

I fell in love with chicken and dumplings when I lived in Atlanta. There was a neighborhood diner that served the dish radiating the kind of heat that has you warming your hands over it. I often ordered it at the end of a waitressing shift to bring me back to life. The chicken soup part was okay, but the pillowy dumplings fascinated me. I was blown away by the idea of biscuits cooked in soup! After several bites, I thought about adding them to *pollo en fricasé*, which is Puerto Rican comfort food at its finest. That dish is typically made with bone-in chicken braised in a tomato sauce with white wine or beer and dotted with the briny pop of alcaparrado, a jarred mixture of pitted Spanish olives, pimentos, and capers. For me, this makes a much more flavorful base for dumplings. And so, my Fricasé Chicken and Dumplings was born.

To save time, use store-bought biscuit dough. If you're vegetarian, substitute the chicken and chicken stock with plant-based options.

SERVES 6

- 2 pounds boneless, skinless chicken thighs, cut into 2-inch chunks (fat discarded) (sub with plant-based chicken for a vegetarian preparation)
- 2 teaspoons Adobo (page 30)
- 1 tablespoon distilled white vinegar
- 2 tablespoons Annatto Oil (page 37), divided
- ½ cup Recaíto (page 34)
- 1 cup plain tomato sauce
- 3 cups chicken stock or broth (sub with vegetable broth for a vegetarian preparation)
- 1 russet potato, peeled and cut into a large dice
- 1 large carrot, peeled or scrubbed well, and cut in ½-inch rounds
- ½ cup store-bought alcaparrado
- 1 bay leaf
- 1 teaspoon kosher salt, plus more as needed

1. In a large mixing bowl, combine the chicken, Adobo, vinegar, and 1 tablespoon of the Annatto Oil and toss until thoroughly coated. Cover and marinate in the refrigerator for at least 1 hour and no more than 24 hours.

2. Heat the remaining tablespoon of Annatto Oil in a large cast-iron skillet or heavy ovenproof sauté pan, over medium high heat, until it shimmers. Working in batches, add the marinated chicken pieces and cook just long enough to brown them lightly (they will not be cooked through). Discard any remaining marinade.

3. Add the Recaíto, stirring to incorporate. Cook for about 1 minute, or until fragrant and bubbling, then stir in the tomato sauce. Cook for 3 minutes, or until the mixture thickens.

4. Stir in the stock, then add the potato, carrot, alcaparrado, and bay leaf. If the stock is unsalted, add the salt. Raise the mixture to a full boil, then reduce the heat to low, cover, and cook for about 30 minutes, or until the liquid reduces further (the vegetables will not be cooked through). Taste and add more salt as needed, being mindful that, as it cooks in the oven, the liquid will reduce further, increasing its saltiness.

5. Meanwhile, make the dumplings: In a large mixing bowl, whisk together the flour, baking powder, and salt. In a liquid measuring cup, stir together the buttermilk and egg, then add the melted butter. Pour into the flour mixture, stirring to form a shaggy dough.

6. Preheat the oven to 425°F.

7. When the fricasé is ready, uncover the pot and discard the bay leaf. Using cooking oil spray to grease a soup spoon, use that spoon to gently drop heaping portions of dough on top of the fricasé. This should yield about 12 dumplings. Scatter the chilled butter evenly over the dumplings.

8. Transfer to the oven and bake, uncovered, for 20 to 30 minutes, until the dumplings are fluffy, golden, and cooked through, and the fricasé is bubbling, with tender vegetables and chicken. Cool slightly before serving in wide, shallow bowls.

Dumplings

1½ cups all-purpose flour

1½ teaspoons baking powder

½ teaspoon kosher salt

¾ cup buttermilk, preferably full-fat

1 large egg

2 tablespoons (¼ stick) salted butter, melted and cooled, plus 1 tablespoon (⅛ stick) chilled salted butter, cut into cubes

Cooking oil spray

COCONUT MILK CLAM CHOWDER

I've had a soft spot for Campbell's New England Clam Chowder since the first time my dad let it glop out of the can in his little trailer park kitchen. Though I was disgusted at first, after two minutes in the microwave, it was love at first bite. This is my Spanglish take on a childhood favorite. You can use peeled fresh yuca, or frozen and thawed yuca. I prefer frozen for convenience. Just make sure to remove the woody center root that runs through the length of the yuca, as it doesn't break down. You won't find a measurement for salt in this recipe, as the amount of salt you will need to use to season your water, will depend on how much water you are using. Generally, try about a tablespoon of kosher salt per gallon of water.

SERVES 6 (MAKES 9 CUPS)

Kosher salt

2 dozen littleneck clams

2 cups yuca root, peeled, woody center removed, cut into ½-inch dice

4 ounces salt pork, cut into a small dice (1 packed cup; may substitute pancetta)

2 tablespoons all-purpose flour

2 tablespoons Recaíto (page 34)

½ cup dry white wine, like a Sauvignon Blanc

1 (13-ounce) can unsweetened coconut milk, well shaken

Finely grated zest and juice of 4 limes (about ¼ cup of juice)

2 (6.5-ounce) cans chopped clams in juice

Freshly ground black pepper

Cilantro leaves, for garnish

1. In a bowl of cool salted water, submerge the clams and soak for 20 minutes to purge them of any grit. Drain and set aside.

2. In a medium pot, bring salted water to a boil over medium-high heat. Add the yuca and boil for 6 to 7 minutes, until tender. Drain and set aside.

3. In a large saucepan, cook the salt pork over medium heat for about 5 minutes, or until its fat has rendered and the pork has crisped. Add the flour and form a paste (roux) with the fat in the pan. Cook for 2 to 3 minutes, until it begins to bubble gently. Add the Recaíto and cook for 1 to 2 minutes, until fragrant.

4. Add the wine and cook for about 3 minutes, or until the liquid has reduced by half. As it reduces, scrape the bottom of the pot to dislodge any browned bits. Add the coconut milk and lime juice. Once the liquid begins to simmer, add the cooked yuca, the littleneck clams, and chopped clams with their juices; make sure the littlenecks are all submerged. Cover and cook for 5 to 7 minutes, until those clams open.

5. Uncover and discard any clams that did not open. Season the chowder with salt and pepper to taste.

6. Garnish each portion with a touch of lime zest and a little cilantro.

SPANGLISH MINESTRONE

Most of the minestrone I had growing up came out of a can and was warmed in a microwave. I'd brighten it with a splash of distilled white vinegar from the bottle that never left our kitchen countertop. Then I'd add a few drops from the bottle of olive oil that always stood next to it like its partner in crime. They transformed the metallic taste of the soup into something zippy. With these canned soups, I often wondered where the Puerto Rican beans were, especially the tender garbanzos I loved to bite into. Here, I've enriched the classic vegetable soup with some of the ingredients my abuela would put in my *sopitas*.

It's easy to make this hearty soup vegetarian by substituting the chicken stock with vegetable stock. The flavors deepen the longer you let it sit, so try making it a day ahead. To store, let the soup cool and place it in an airtight container for up to three days in the fridge and up to three months in the freezer.

SERVES 8 (MAKES ABOUT 14 CUPS)

- 2 tablespoons Annatto Oil (page 37)
- 1 cup Recaíto (page 34)
- 1 small yellow onion, diced (about 1 cup)
- 1 (15-ounce) can whole peeled San Marzano tomatoes, coarsely chopped, with their juices
- 6 cups (1½ quarts) chicken stock or broth
- 1 (15-ounce) can red kidney beans, drained and rinsed
- 1 (15-ounce) can chickpeas, drained and rinsed
- 1 (15-ounce) can gandules, drained and rinsed
- 2 cups peeled yautía root, cut into a small dice (you may find yautía labeled malanga; substitute with yuca, taro, or sweet potato)
- 1 bay leaf
- 1 cup dried pastina (small star-shaped pasta; may substitute with alphabet pasta or acini de pepe)
- 2 tablespoons finely chopped fresh cilantro leaves, plus 2 tablespoons whole cilantro leaves
- 1 chayote, peeled and cut into ½-inch dice (may substitute with summer squash)
- 3 (packed) cups fresh baby spinach, coarsely chopped
- 4 tablespoons grated Parmigiano-Reggiano cheese
- Kosher salt and freshly ground black pepper

1. In a large pot, heat the Annatto Oil over medium heat until it shimmers. Add the Recaíto and onion and cook for about 5 minutes, or until the mixture thickens. Add the tomatoes with their juices and cook for about 10 minutes, or until most of the liquid has evaporated. Add the stock, red kidney beans, chickpeas, gandules, yautía, and bay leaf. Cook for 30 minutes, then discard the bay leaf. The yautía should be barely tender.

2. Stir in the pastina, finely chopped cilantro, and the chayote. Cook for about 5 minutes, or until the chayote has begun to soften, then add the spinach and, stirring occasionally, cook for about 5 minutes, or until it has wilted and all the vegetables are tender.

3. Stir in the whole cilantro leaves and cheese. Season with salt and pepper to taste before serving.

STAUB

Spanglish Minestrone, page 113

PICADILLO CHILI

Like many of my continental favorites, my first taste of chili came via school lunch. I was in second grade, and as I stood waiting in the lunch line, I spied ground beef being scooped into beige plastic bowls. I was sure I was about to have a bowl full of Puerto Rican *picadillo*, a ground beef mixed with olives, capers, raisins, and prunes. I was disappointed when, upon closer inspection, I realized the picadillo was missing about ten ingredients and, for some reason, was floating in tomato sauce. Though I liked the chili, I was overwhelmed with a longing for the flavors of my island and for my abuela, who would make picadillo two or three times a week.

This recipe calls for a lot of ingredients, but the layering of flavors and textures is unbeatable. Picadillo's sweet and savory elements are a perfect example of one of the most important flavor profiles in Puerto Rican cuisine, *agridulce* (savory-sweet). It might sound absolutely bonkers in a chili until you taste it for the first time. Trust!

You can make this recipe vegan by substituting the ground beef with a plant-based option, the beef stock with veggie broth, and the cheese and sour cream with nondairy versions.

SERVES 6
(MAKES ABOUT 9 CUPS)

- 1 tablespoon plus 1½ teaspoons Annatto Oil (page 37)
- 1 pound 80/20 ground beef
- 1 teaspoon kosher salt
- ½ teaspoon Sazón (page 33)
- 1 cup Recaíto (page 34)
- 1 cup plain tomato sauce
- ½ teaspoon dried oregano
- ½ cup alcaparrado
- ¼ cup dark raisins
- 2 tablespoons distilled white vinegar
- 1½ cups beef stock or broth
- 1 (15-ounce) can petite diced tomatoes with their juices
- 1 (15-ounce) can red kidney beans, drained and rinsed
- 1 cup frozen/defrosted baked plantains, cut into a small dice
- ½ cup shredded sharp cheddar cheese, for garnish
- Sour cream, for garnish

1. In a large sauté pan, heat the Annatto Oil over medium heat until it shimmers. Add the beef to the pan in batches and season with the salt and Sazón. Use a spoon to break up any big chunks as the beef browns. Once the beef has been browned, add the Recaíto and tomato sauce. Cook for about 5 minutes, or until bubbling, occasionally stirring.

2. Add the oregano, alcaparrado, raisins, vinegar, stock, diced tomatoes and their juices, and the beans. Bring to a boil then reduce the heat to medium-low. Cook, uncovered, for 20 to 25 minutes, stirring occasionally, until the chili thickens.

3. Remove from the heat and stir in the plantains. Let the chili cool for a few minutes before serving. Garnish each portion with the cheese and a dollop of sour cream.

CREAM OF YAUTÍA
WITH PANCETTA

Yautía, also known as malanga, is a starchy root vegetable that's part of the group of root vegetables many Puerto Ricans refer to as *viandas*. It's often boiled in big chunks on the island and served with other viandas. It has an earthy, nutty flavor that pairs excellently with buttery cream and becomes even more pronounced when dotted with salty pancetta.

You can make this recipe vegan by substituting the chicken stock with veggie stock and the heavy cream and milk with coconut cream and coconut milk. Sub the pancetta with fried chopped mushrooms.

SERVES 8 (MAKES ABOUT 7 CUPS)

1½ pounds frozen yautía, if using fresh, peel and cut into 2-inch chunks (may substitute with taro)

2 tablespoons olive oil, divided

1 teaspoon kosher salt, divided, plus more as needed

1 medium onion, cut into a small dice (about 1 cup)

3 garlic cloves, minced

1 cup chicken stock

½ cup heavy cream

¾ cup whole milk

Pinch of freshly grated nutmeg

8 ounces pancetta, cut into a small dice, for garnish

Handful of cilantro leaves, for garnish

1. Preheat the oven to 450°F.

2. Set an ovenproof wire rack inside a rimmed baking sheet.

3. In a bowl, toss the yautía with 1 tablespoon of the olive oil and ½ teaspoon of the salt, then spread the coated yautía chunks on the rack in a single layer. Roast for about 30 minutes, or until all the yautía has softened and some of it has started to caramelize.

4. Meanwhile, in a large heavy pot, heat the remaining tablespoon of oil over medium-high heat until it shimmers. Stir in the onion and the remaining ½ teaspoon salt. Cook for about 5 minutes, or until translucent. Add the garlic and cook for about 1 minute, or until fragrant.

5. Add 4 cups water and the stock; once the liquid comes to a boil, add the roasted yautía. Reduce the heat to medium and cook, uncovered, for about 10 minutes, or until the liquid is bubbling and the yautía falls apart when a fork is pressed into it. Remove from the heat.

6. Let the yautía cool slightly. With a slotted spoon, transfer half of it to a blender with 2 cups cooking liquid; reserve the rest. Remove the lid plug and cover the opening with a towel to vent steam. Purée to a smooth, gravy-like texture, adding liquid as needed. Do not over-blend to avoid a gluey texture.

7. Add the remaining yautía and enough liquid to maintain the gravy-like consistency. Set aside any unused liquid in the pot and return all of the puree to the pot. (Unused yautía water can be frozen in ice cube trays and used to thicken gluten-free gravies.)

8. Over medium heat, add the heavy cream, milk, and the pinch of nutmeg; cook, uncovered, for about 10 minutes, or until the soup is bubbling and glossy, stirring a few times. Taste, and add more salt as needed.

9. Meanwhile, place the pancetta in a small nonstick skillet, over medium-low heat. Cook for about 8 minutes, or until the fat renders and the pancetta crisps. Drain the bits on a paper towel.

10. Serve the soup hot, garnished with the crisped pancetta and cilantro.

SOFRITO TOMATO SOUP

SERVES 6 (MAKES ABOUT 10 CUPS)

Let's just say that when it comes to canned tomato soup, it has never been a love story. For me, it tastes metallic and flat and the texture is just shy of tomato sauce. This soup, on the other hand, is vibrant, mesmerizing, and always leaves you wanting more. The sofrito base gives it an intensely flavored foundation without masking the tomato, and the coconut milk adds body and creaminess.

If you want to make a vegan version of this recipe, use plant-based butter, sub the salt pork in the Sofrito with a teaspoon of white miso, and use veggie broth.

- 8 tablespoons (1 stick) salted butter
- 2 medium yellow onions, cut into ½-inch dice (about 2 cups)
- 1 teaspoon Adobo (page 30)
- 1 teaspoon Sazón (page 33)
- ½ teaspoon kosher salt, plus more as needed
- ¼ teaspoon freshly ground black pepper, plus more as needed
- 1 cup Sofrito (page 38)
- 3 tablespoons all-purpose flour
- 2 (28-ounce) cans whole, crushed San Marzano tomatoes, plus their juices
- 1 cup chicken stock or broth
- 1 cup coconut milk, well shaken

1. In a Dutch oven or large heavy pot, melt the butter over medium heat. Add the onions, Adobo, Sazón, salt, and pepper. Cook for about 10 minutes, or until the onions are translucent, stirring often.
2. Stir in the Sofrito. Cook, stirring, for about 4 minutes, or until the mixture thickens and darkens in color.
3. Stir in the flour and cook for about 2 minutes to form a chunky paste with no trace of dry flour; scrape the bottom of the pot a few times to prevent sticking.
4. Add the tomatoes and their juices, the stock, and coconut milk. Stir until the mixture begins to simmer. Reduce the heat to low, partially cover, and cook for 20 minutes, stirring occasionally to prevent sticking. Remove from the heat.
5. Allow it to cool for a few minutes; once the soup is no longer simmering, use an immersion (stick) blender to puree it until fairly smooth (or your desired consistency). Alternatively, remove the cap from the center of your blender lid and place a towel over the opening (so steam can escape from the hot contents). Puree in batches, and return them to the pot.
6. Taste and add more salt and/or pepper as needed. Once the pureed soup is heated through, divide it among individual bowls and serve.

On the Side

Snacks, Starters, and Salads

MEZCLA DEVILED EGGS

My mother loved to entertain and served platters of little sandwiches *"de mezcla"* to her friends and family as they swapped *bochinche* (gossip). Crusts were cut off the white bread, and the sandwiches were quartered, making them perfect finger food for a six-year-old. At these parties, the sandwiches were always the first to run out, so I made sure to stuff extras in my pocket before heading off to a corner to chow down. I had no idea that the pinkish spread that I loved so much was a mix of Spam, roasted red peppers, and canned cheese.

Mezcla is a nostalgic bite that instantly takes me back to the island, and using it as stuffing for deviled eggs is truly a knockout. I know blending Spam and nacho cheese with hard-cooked egg yolks sounds crazy, but just try it.

SERVES 6

¼ cup nacho cheese dip, at room temperature

4 tablespoons cream cheese, at room temperature

¼ cup jarred or canned pimentos, juice reserved

1 tablespoon chopped Calabrian chili peppers

½ can (6 ounces) Spam, cut into cubes

18 large eggs, preferably at room temperature

Hot smoked paprika, for garnish

1. Bring a large pot of water to a boil over high heat. Meanwhile, in a food processor, combine the nacho cheese dip, cream cheese, pimentos, Calabrian chili peppers, and Spam. Puree until velvety smooth.

2. Once the pot of water is boiling, remove it from the heat. Use a ladle or slotted spoon to carefully add the eggs to the hot water. Cover the pot and let the eggs sit for 12 minutes.

3. Fill a large bowl with water and ice cubes and transfer the eggs there. Once they have cooled, peel the eggs and cut them in half lengthwise. Remove the yolks, adding them to the mixture in the food processor along with 1 tablespoon of the pimentos' juice. Puree until smooth. If the filling seems too thick, add an additional tablespoon of pimento juice.

4. Arrange the egg white halves on a plate (you may need to trim their bottoms a bit, so they sit flat).

5. Fit a piping bag with a star tip. Add the mezcla deviled egg mixture to the bag. Fill each egg white half with some of the mezcla deviled egg mixture. Garnish each one with a sprinkle of paprika.

BACALAÍTO-BATTERED ONION RINGS

Bacalaítos are crispy, greasy, salty, and my absolute favorite *fritura* (fried food). They are made by frying scoops of a savory batter dotted with salted codfish. Fresh bacalaíto batter is a bit labor-intensive to make, but if you're game, I have a recipe for you. Bacalaíto batter from scratch isn't always in the cards for me. That's why I use boxed bacalaíto mix for these onion rings. Serve with Spicy Mayo-Ketchup (page 42).

SERVES 4

- Corn, canola, or vegetable oil, for frying
- 2 (4.5-ounce) packages bacalaíto mix, aka codfish fritter mix (or try my recipe on page 126)
- 1 (12-ounce) bottle light-colored beer, such as Medalla, Miller, or Pabst
- 1 cup all-purpose flour, plus more as needed
- ½ cup rice flour, plus more as needed
- 2 large yellow onions

1. In a Dutch oven or other large heavy pot, pour in oil to a depth of 2 inches. Bring to 375°F over medium-high heat, using an instant-read thermometer to monitor the temperature.

2. In a medium bowl, combine the bacalaíto mix and the beer, stirring to form a lump-free batter. Let it sit for 10 to 15 minutes; it will thicken. In a separate bowl, mix the all-purpose flour and rice flour.

3. Meanwhile, place a baking sheet in the oven and preheat to 200°F.

4. Cut the onions horizontally into 1-inch-thick rings. You should have about 3 cups. Toss a few at a time in the flour until evenly coated.

5. Dip the onion rings one by one into the rested batter. If they aren't completely coated, you may need to toss them in the flour again, and then recoat them in the batter. Add flour to the bowl as needed.

6. Use tongs to carefully lay the rings away from you into the hot oil, which should bubble around them. Watch closely and cook for less than a minute, just until the onion rings are golden brown.

7. Line another baking sheet with paper towels and place a wire rack over it. Use tongs to transfer the fried onion rings to the rack to drain. Once your next batch of battered onion rings is in the hot oil, transfer the drained onion rings to the oven to keep warm.

8. Discard any leftover flour and batter.

BACALAÍTOS

Bacalaítos are my favorite Puerto Rican street food. I love buying them at ramshackle beach kiosks where I can watch them get fried (â la minute) in large vats of furiously bubbling oil. They are crispy, golden-brown fritters made up of tiny flakes of salt cod suspended in a flavorful batter. Think of them like savory salt-cod pancakes that are made freeform, so they can be hand-size or bigger than a dinner plate. They are salty, crunchy, and unctuous. Eat them as is or serve them with a variety of sauces, like my Spicy Mayo-Ketchup, Salsa Criolla (page 49), or Ajilimójili (page 46).

SERVES 4

½ pound salt cod

1 cup rice flour

1 teaspoon baking powder

1 tablespoon cornstarch

1 teaspoon Sazón (page 33)

¼ teaspoon Adobo (page 30)

1 (12-ounce) bottle light-colored beer, such as Medalla, Miller, or Pabst for thinning the batter

2 tablespoons minced onion

1 teaspoon minced garlic

1 tablespoon Sofrito (page 38)

1 teaspoon white vinegar

2 cups canola oil

Spicy Mayo-Ketchup (page 42), for dipping

1. Rinse the salt cod under running water really well. Then soak it in a big pot of fresh, cool water for 30 minutes. Drain the water and soak the cod again in fresh water for an additional 30 minutes.
2. Drain the water out of the pot a second time and cover the salt cod again in fresh water. Place the pot over medium heat and simmer the cod for 30 minutes. Drain the cod again.
3. Let the cod sit until it's cool enough to work with, then use a fork to flake it apart. Make sure to get rid of any bones you find.
4. **Make the batter:** In a medium bowl, mix the rice flour, baking powder, cornstarch, Sazón, and Adobo. Add 1 cup beer, little by little, mixing until it looks like runny pancake batter; add more beer as needed to get to this consistency. Add the onion, garlic, Sofrito, vinegar, and cod. Mix well.
5. Line a plate with paper towels. In a frying pan, using an instant-read thermometer, heat the oil to 350°F. Carefully ladle in anywhere from ¼ cup to ½ cup of the batter into the hot oil. These are just like pancakes, the more batter you ladle in, the bigger they are.
6. Fry the bacalaítos for 2 minutes, or until golden, then flip. Fry them for a few minutes more, or until crispy and golden brown.
7. Drain the bacalaítos on the paper towel-lined plate. When they've cooled, eat them as is or dip them in Spicy Mayo-Ketchup!

SCALLOPED VIANDAS
WITH ESCABECHE

Viandas is the umbrella term for Puerto Rican starchy roots and tubers such as yuca, malanga, taro, and sweet potatoes. And though they grow on trees, green plantains are also considered a vianda. In this Spanglish recipe, I replace the commonly used potato with tropical roots and tubers and drizzle them with a tart and briny Escabeche (page 45) instead of cheese.

Serve these Scalloped Viandas with Escabeche with a Tamarind Roast Chicken (page 145) or as a side for Lamb Picadillo Meatloaf (page 142).

SERVES 8

Cooking oil spray

Kosher salt

1 large yautía (about 1 pound), peeled and cut into ¼-inch rounds (you may find yautía labeled malanga; substitute with yuca, taro, or sweet potato)

1 large ñame or yam (about 1 pound), peeled and cut into ¼-inch rounds

1 large yuca (about 1 pound), peeled and woody center discarded, cut into ¼-inch half-moons

4 tablespoons (½ stick) salted butter

1 medium yellow onion, cut into a small dice (about 1 cup)

2 cups whole milk or coconut milk

1 cup vegetable broth

¼ cup all-purpose flour

¼ teaspoon freshly ground black pepper

Pinch of freshly grated nutmeg

½ teaspoon Adobo (page 30)

Pinch of ground cayenne pepper

Escabeche (page 45), for serving

1. Use cooking oil spray to grease a 9-inch-square casserole dish or another 2-quart baking dish. Set aside.

2. Fill a large pot halfway with cool water and stir in enough salt (about 1 tablespoon per gallon) so the water will taste like the ocean. Add the sliced viandas (yautía, ñame, and yuca); this will help prevent them from turning brown.

3. Place the pot over medium-high heat. Bring to a boil and cook the sliced viandas for 1 to 2 minutes, just until they have started to soften. Drain the viandas in a colander, discarding the water. Let cool.

4. In a heavy saucepan, over medium heat, melt the butter. Stir in the onion and cook for about 5 minutes, or until translucent.

5. Meanwhile, preheat the oven to 350°F.

6. Combine the whole milk and broth in a microwave-safe container; microwave (100% power) for about 1 minute, or just until barely steaming.

7. Sprinkle the flour over the diced onion in the saucepan and cook for about 2 minutes, stirring until no visible flour remains, to form a paste.

8. Raise the heat to medium-high; add the hot milk and broth, stirring until a thickened sauce forms. Once the mixture begins to bubble, add ¼ teaspoon salt, the black pepper, pinch of nutmeg, Adobo, and pinch of cayenne pepper. Reduce the heat to medium-low, and cook for 2 minutes more. Remove from the heat.

9. To assemble, spoon a thin layer of sauce at the bottom of the prepared casserole or baking dish. Next, layer a third of the par-cooked viandas and cover with a third of the sauce. Repeat two more times, using all the viandas and ending with the sauce. Cover the dish tightly with aluminum foil, place on a baking sheet, and bake for 40 minutes, then uncover and bake for 40 to 50 minutes more, until the sauce is bubbly and golden brown on top, and a knife is inserted into the viandas meets no resistance.

10. Serve hot. Top each portion with a few tablespoons of Escabeche.

CARIBBEAN COWBOY CAVIAR

My abuelo grew bell peppers on our finca. He walked my brother and me to the patch next to our tin-roofed farm a few times a week to watch them get bigger and bigger. They transformed over the course of a couple of weeks from vivid green to stop-sign red. Even though he asked me not to, I couldn't help but run my finger along their ridges. It always earned me an irritated "*¡Carajo!*"

Making anything with red bell peppers always reminds me of my abuelo, and maybe that's why this salad is so special to me. It's got great texture, with loads of crunch from the fresh peppers, a pop of honey from the mango, and earthiness from the cilantro. This is a great cookout salad as it racks up the compliments, feeds loads of people, and is easy to put together. Open a few cans, cut up some produce, and you're basically done. Feel free to substitute the honey mangoes with whatever mangoes you can score—even high-quality frozen ones will do the trick; defrost and taste them before you add them to the salad. You can sweeten it with a drizzle of honey if necessary.

SERVES 6
(MAKES ABOUT
10½ CUPS)

Dressing

3 tablespoons olive oil

Finely grated zest and juice of 1 lime

1 tablespoon Pique (page 41)

1 teaspoon Adobo (page 30)

½ teaspoon kosher salt

½ teaspoon light brown sugar

Salad

1 (15-ounce) can garbanzo beans

1 (15-ounce) can pink beans

1 (15-ounce) can black beans

6 to 7 ounces sweet peppers (red, orange, yellow), seeded, and cut into a small dice

3 Roma tomatoes, hulled, and cut into a small dice

2 honey mangoes (also called Ataulfo mangoes), peeled, seeded, and cut into a small dice

½ medium red onion, cut into a small dice (½ cup)

1 (packed) cup chopped fresh cilantro

Kosher salt

Plantain chips, for serving

1. Make the dressing: In a liquid measuring cup, whisk together the olive oil, 2 tablespoons of lime juice, lime zest, the Pique, Adobo, salt, and brown sugar, until the sugar has dissolved.

2. Make the salad: Line a baking sheet with paper towels. In a colander set in the sink, combine the garbanzo, pink, and black beans. Rinse them well with cool water and drain, then pour them onto the prepared baking sheet and pat dry.

3. In a large bowl, combine the beans, sweet peppers, tomatoes, mangoes, red onion, and cilantro. Pour the dressing around the inside of the bowl and mix gently so the vegetables are evenly coated.

4. Cover and refrigerate until well chilled. Stir and add salt to taste before serving with plantain chips.

MANGO & AVOCADO PANZANELLA SALAD

The trick to amazing panzanella is to give the cubes of day-old bread time to soak up the dressing, transforming their rock-hard texture into chewy flavor bombs with moments of crunch and pockets of acidity. If you're working with fresh bread, cut it into a 2-inch dice and pop it into a 300°F oven for twenty minutes. It will dry out the cubes to create the right texture. I add a Spanglish twist to this Italian salad with diced mango and avocado, grated ginger root, and crumbled queso fresco.

SERVES 6 (MAKES ABOUT 12 CUPS)

- 3 (packed) cups cubed stale crusty artisan bread
- 4 tablespoons olive oil, divided
- 2 ripe honey mangoes (also called Ataulfo mangoes)
- ¼ teaspoon crushed red pepper flakes
- 1 ripe Hass avocado
- 1 tablespoon, plus 1½ teaspoons distilled white vinegar, divided
- 1 pint cherry tomatoes
- 1¼ teaspoons salt, divided
- ½ medium red onion (see Tip)
- 1 (4-ounce block) queso fresco
- 10 ounces baby spring mix greens
- ¼ teaspoon freshly ground black pepper

1. Preheat the oven to 300°F.
2. Line a baking sheet with parchment paper. Cut the bread into 2-inch cubes and spread it in a single layer on the prepared baking sheet. Drizzle with 1 tablespoon of the olive oil and toss to lightly coat. Bake for about 15 minutes, or until crisped and lightly browned. Let cool on the sheet.
3. Peel and pit the mangoes. Cut the flesh into ½-inch chunks and season them with the crushed red pepper flakes. Pit the avocado and discard the skin; cut the flesh into ½-inch chunks and drizzle them with the 1½ teaspoons of the vinegar (to help keep them from discoloring). Cut each cherry tomato in half and season the halves with ¼ teaspoon of the salt. Cut the red onion into half-moons ¼ inch thick. Cut the queso fresco into ½-inch chunks.
4. Transfer the toasted bread cubes to a large bowl Top with the greens, then the tomatoes, mango, avocado, red onion, and queso fresco.
5. In a small jar with a tight-fitting lid, combine the remaining 3 tablespoons of olive oil, the 1 tablespoon of vinegar, the remaining teaspoon of salt, and the black pepper. Seal and shake to form an emulsified dressing.
6. At least 1 hour before serving, pour the dressing over the salad and toss to coat evenly.

TIP: To soften the bite of raw red onion, soak the half-moons in cool water for a few minutes then rinse.

CRISPY COCONUT RICE

In Spanish, *pegao* means "stuck" and it is everything when it comes to Puerto Rican rice. Pegao is how we refer to the crispy bits of rice that stick to the bottom of the pot and must be scraped out. People will fight over pegao. Abuelas will chastise you over the fat you use to make it. (The old-school way is oil and never butter.) Arguments will erupt over who took too much and what it says about their character. When it hits the table, it's the first thing everyone pops in their mouth, and it's only then that no one says a word because they're too busy chewing.

This recipe is inspired by the glutton in me. I wanted to increase the output of crispy rice, and also scent it and make it creamier. Nothing about this preparation is traditional and is sure to send the Boricua food police into a rage. I don't care. Crispy Coconut Rice is fantastic. It pairs well with Hibiscus Baked Beans (page 135) and Jackfruit Ropa Vieja (page 152). Refrigerate the rice in an airtight container for up to three days. To warm, sprinkle with a touch of water and reheat until steaming.

SERVES 4

- 1 cup coconut milk, well shaken
- ½ cup water
- 2 teaspoons kosher salt
- 2 cups uncooked medium-grain rice, rinsed until the water runs clear
- 2 tablespoons canola oil

1. In a medium saucepan, combine the coconut milk, ½ cup water, and the salt over high heat. Once the liquid comes to a boil, stir in the rice. Bring back to a boil.

2. Once the rice develops a few steam vents on the surface (about 1 minute after it comes to a boil), stir it well, reduce the heat to medium-low, cover, and cook for about 15 minutes, or until all the liquid has been absorbed and the rice is tender. Remove the pan from the heat and let it sit, covered, for 10 minutes.

3. Uncover and fluff the rice with a fork. Cool for 10 minutes.

4. In a 10-inch cast-iron skillet, heat the oil over high heat until it begins to shimmer. Use a large spatula to carefully add the cooled rice to the pan, and then use the spatula to press the rice down, flattening the surface of the rice. Cover the surface of the rice with a plate and place a heavy can on top of the plate. Cook for 12 to 15 minutes, until the bottom of the rice becomes golden and crisped. Transfer to a platter and serve.

HIBISCUS BAKED BEANS

When my brother and I were toddlers, our neighbor Chanchi often babysat us, so my abuela could leave the farm to run errands in town. Back then, I thought Chanchi might be related to the Jolly Green Giant on the bags of mixed veggies my abuela kept in the freezer. She stood at least eight inches taller than my grandmother. Chanchi had the largest feet I'd ever seen and a beautiful belly that poked out of the T-shirt she was always adjusting.

On hot, humid days, Chanchi made a pink tea she poured into plastic cups that had been washed so much they looked ashy. The tea is *té de Jamaica*, and it's made by steeping dried hibiscus flowers in hot water. It tastes a little like a cranberry walked through the perfume section at Macy's—tart but floral. While I love drinking it as a simple tea, hibiscus makes a fantastic addition to baked beans. I use navy beans, or *habichuelas blancas*, which in Puerto Rico we commonly use for stew. They hold their shape well during a long cook, and they win me over with their tender, creamy texture. Try them served over Crispy Coconut Rice (page 132). They pair wonderfully with Tamarind Roast Chicken (page 145).

SERVES 8 (MAKES ABOUT 8 CUPS)

- 1 tablespoon vegetable, corn, or canola oil
- 1 medium onion, cut into a small dice (about 1 cup)
- 1½ cups Sofrito (page 38), or store-bought
- 1 (15-ounce) can crushed tomatoes
- 3½ cups chicken stock or broth, divided
- 1 tablespoon distilled white vinegar
- 1 tablespoon Worcestershire sauce
- 1 cup (40 grams) dried hibiscus flowers
- ¼ (packed) cup light brown sugar
- 1 teaspoon Sazón (page 33)
- 2 teaspoons kosher salt
- ¼ teaspoon freshly ground black pepper
- 1 bay leaf
- 3 (15-ounce) cans navy beans, drained and rinsed

1. Preheat the oven to 325°F.
2. In a large cast-iron skillet or oven-proof, heavy pot, heat the vegetable oil over medium heat until it shimmers. Add the onion and cook for about 5 minutes, or until translucent.
3. Add the Sofrito and cook for about 5 minutes, or until thickened. Add the crushed tomatoes and cook for about 5 minutes, or until bubbling and thickened. Add 1½ cups of the stock, the vinegar, Worcestershire sauce, hibiscus flowers, brown sugar, Sazón, salt, pepper, and bay leaf. Cook for 20 minutes, stirring occasionally to prevent sticking.
4. Remove the bay leaf. Add the sauce to a high-powered blender jar and cover with a towel instead of the blender lid, so steam doesn't build up. Puree the tomato mixture into a smooth paste. Add back to the pan and stir in the remaining 2 cups of stock until thoroughly incorporated.
5. Stir in the beans, then transfer to the oven and bake for 30 minutes.
6. Stir the hot mixture and continue to bake for about 30 minutes more, or until the sauce has thickened and darkened in color. Serve warm.

ROASTED GREEN PAPAYA & CARROTS

We had a cluster of papaya trees on our farm in Boquerón, and our farmhand Lelo would pick their fruit when they were heavy and bright orange. Upon picking them, he sliced the papayas open with his machete and scooped out their pearly black seeds with his hands. I hated the way their smell overpowered everything else. Then he chopped them into thick slices and ate them, their juices dribbling down his face and into his hands. He offered us slippery slices, but I always declined, as when my nose got anywhere near them, I had to hold my breath not to puke.

I didn't taste green papaya until I was in my thirties and living in Seattle, next to a Thai restaurant. I loved the crunch, and that it didn't smell like ripe papaya. When it's roasted, green papaya's flavors deepen and create a creamier texture. I love it with carrots, caramelized and drizzled with a tart passion fruit dressing. Pair this salad with Tamarind Roast Chicken (page 145) or Malta-Braised Short Ribs (page 146).

SERVES 8

- 1 medium green papaya (about 2 pounds)
- 1 pound carrots, scrubbed well and each cut in half lengthwise
- 3 tablespoons olive oil, divided
- ½ teaspoon kosher salt, plus more as needed
- ⅛ teaspoon freshly ground black pepper
- ½ cup passion fruit juice
- 1 tablespoon light brown sugar
- 2 teaspoons distilled white vinegar
- About 2 (packed) cups baby arugula
- Finely grated zest and juice of 1 lime, for garnish
- ½ teaspoon peeled, grated fresh ginger root, for garnish
- ¼ cup roasted, salted pepitas (pumpkin seeds), for garnish

1. Preheat the oven to 400°F.
2. Peel the papaya, cut in half lengthwise, and remove the seeds. Cut the flesh into 1-inch-thick slices.
3. Line a rimmed baking sheet with parchment paper. Spread the carrots and papaya on the baking sheet in a single layer. Drizzle with 2 tablespoons of the olive oil and toss to coat thoroughly. Season with the salt and pepper. Roast for 50 to 60 minutes, until they are tender and nicely browned on the bottom.
4. Meanwhile, in a small saucepan, over medium-high heat, combine the passion fruit juice, brown sugar, and vinegar. Cook for a few minutes, until reduced by half to form a glaze. Remove from the heat.
5. Brush the glaze over the carrots and papaya, return them to the oven, and roast for about 5 minutes more, or until they look caramelized. Transfer them to a platter.
6. Scatter the arugula evenly over the warm caramelized carrots and papaya. Drizzle the arugula with the remaining tablespoon of oil. The arugula will wilt slightly.
7. Drizzle the lime juice over the arugula and finish with a pinch of salt. Sprinkle the lime zest, ginger, and pepitas over the entire platter and serve warm.

TIP: **Save the papaya seeds and rinse them thoroughly. Spread them out in a single layer on a paper towel, then microwave in 30-second bursts until completely dry, about 2 minutes total. Once cooled, grind the dried seeds into a coarse, aromatic "pepper."**

Main Squeezes

Meat, Seafood, and Vegetarian Dishes

BUCATINI
WITH CLAM AJILIMÓJILI

On the days when my abuelo approached us with our brightly colored beach buckets and shovels in hand, my brother and I knew we were in for a treat. We slipped on our dirty *chanclas* (flip flops) and ran to the marshy strip by the shore to dig for clams during low tide. My abuelo wasn't much of a talker, but during these outings, he mumbled to himself in a steady stream as if trying to start a conversation with the clam colony he was searching for. His movements over the sandy marsh were swift, stopping occasionally to stomp his feet, stare, and curse. He studied the ankle-deep water closely before he set us to digging. Within a minute or two, we had tiny white-shelled clams in our hands. This process continued until we had filled our buckets (and our ears with new strings of cursing possibilities). He rinsed the clams in the still turquoise saltwater of our beach and took them to my abuela to prepare over our *fogón* (wood-burning stove).

Canned clams are a far cry from the fresh clams of my childhood, but they work for this quick weeknight meal. Simmering them in garlicky ajilimójili masks any metallic notes and serving them over bucatini turns this into a hearty dinner. You can, of course, use whatever pasta you have on hand. If you have leftovers or if you want to make the clam sauce ahead of time, refrigerate it in an airtight container for up to five days or freeze for up to three months.

SERVES 4

Kosher salt

1 pound dried bucatini pasta

1 cup Ajilimójili (page 46)

2 (10-ounce) cans chopped clams, with their juices

¼ (packed) cup chopped flat-leaf parsley, for garnish

½ cup grated Parmigiano-Reggiano cheese, for garnish

TIP: Any remaining pasta water can be frozen in ice cube trays and used to thicken sauces or soups. It also makes incredibly fluffy scrambled eggs.

1. Fill a large, deep saucepan three-quarters full with water and bring to a boil over medium-high heat. Add enough salt so the water tastes like the ocean, approximately 1 tablespoon per gallon of water.

2. Add the bucatini and cook for about 2 minutes less than directed on the package. Reserve a ½ cup of the pasta cooking water before draining the bucatini in a colander set in the sink.

3. Meanwhile, in a separate large saucepan, over medium heat, warm through the Ajilimójili for about 2 minutes, or until fragrant and bubbling. Add the clams and two-thirds of their juices; add the final third of the juices to the reserved pasta cooking water. Cook for 8 to 10 minutes, or until the juices have reduced by half.

4. Add the bucatini to the pan. Stir to coat and cook for 2 minutes. If the sauce doesn't quite come together or if there's not enough to coat the pasta well, add a few tablespoons of the reserved pasta cooking water (see Tip).

5. Serve warm and garnish with the parsley and cheese.

LAMB PICADILLO MEATLOAF

My mother went through a meatloaf phase when my brother and I were eight years old and had just moved to Houston. She made it a few times a week for a couple of months, as if conquering a traditional recipe from the Lower 48 would help us fit in. But you can't take the *extra* out of a Latina and nothing basic ever came out of her kitchen. She stuffed hard-boiled eggs in her meatloaf, and sometimes chopped ham. One time she made it with olives, and the slices looked like they were staring at us. We stared back at them just as hard.

I channeled my mother when I created this recipe. This Lamb Picadillo Meatloaf is just as *extra*. I invert the pan during the bake, a trick I learned from food science genius J. Kenji López-Alt. It's a few extra steps. But it's worth it. It increases the amount of area you can glaze, rewarding you with loads of deeply flavored caramelization. Make it for a special occasion and rack up the compliments.

SERVES 6 (MAKES ONE 9 X 5-INCH LOAF)

Meatloaf

2 tablespoons olive oil

1 cup Sofrito (page 38)

¼ cup plain tomato sauce

2 teaspoons Worcestershire sauce

1 teaspoon Sazón (page 33)

¼ cup buttermilk, preferably full-fat

¼ cup fruity red wine, such as Merlot or Malbec

¼ cup chicken stock or broth

½ cup panko breadcrumbs

1 pound 80/20 ground pork

1 pound 80/20 ground lamb

2 large eggs

¼ cup grated Parmigiano-Reggiano cheese

¼ cup minced flat-leaf parsley, plus more for garnish

1 tablespoon kosher salt, plus more as needed

1 teaspoon freshly ground black pepper, plus more as needed

¼ cup dark raisins

¼ cup sliced pimento-stuffed Spanish or Manzanilla olives

1. **Make the meatloaf:** In a deep sauté pan, heat the olive oil over medium heat until it shimmers. Add the Sofrito and cook for about 2 minutes, or until fragrant. Stir in the tomato sauce, Worcestershire sauce, and Sazón; cook for about 5 minutes, or until the mixture thickens.

2. Stir in the buttermilk, wine, and stock. Cook for about 8 minutes, or until the liquid has reduced by half, adjusting the heat as needed. (The buttermilk may look a bit curdled; that's okay.)

3. Stir in the panko until well incorporated, then transfer the contents to a bowl and cool to room temperature. The yield is about 1¾ cups.

4. Meanwhile, combine the pork and lamb in the bowl of a stand mixer fitted with the paddle attachment. Mix on the lowest speed for about 20 seconds until well incorporated. (If you don't have a stand mixer, use a whole lot of elbow grease, and mix the ingredients in this step and the next one by hand in a large bowl.)

5. Add the eggs, cheese, parsley, salt, and pepper. Mix on the lowest speed until fully blended. Remove the bowl from the stand mixer and fold in the cooled panko mixture along with the raisins and olives until evenly distributed.

6. To taste for seasoning, in a small skillet over medium heat, cook a little of the meatloaf mixture for a minute or two. Add more salt and/or pepper to the remaining meatloaf mixture as needed.

7. Transfer the mixture to a 9 x 5-inch loaf pan. Eliminate any air pockets by knocking the pan on the counter a few times, then use a skewer or chopstick to create 6 holes (for steam and even cooking), poking all the way to the bottom of the pan. Smooth the surface, all the way to the corners. Wrap the pan in a sheet of aluminum foil that's big enough to cover the top and sides (top, folded under the bottom), and refrigerate for 15 minutes.

8. Preheat the oven to 350°F. Line a quarter baking sheet with foil. Invert the chilled meatloaf in its loaf pan onto the baking sheet. Loosen the foil around the pan just enough so that the edges will catch the meatloaf's juices as it bakes.

9. Bake for 30 minutes, then use a metal spatula to lift an edge of the pan off the loaf. The meatloaf should be set. If it is, remove the baking sheet from the oven just long enough to remove the loaf pan and drain some of the fat collecting in the foil. The internal temperature taken at the center of the loaf should register 140°F; let it rest for 15 minutes. If not, return the uncovered meatloaf to the oven and bake until it does.

10. Raise the oven temperature to broil and adjust your oven racks as needed.

11. Make the glaze: In the same skillet you used for the taste test, combine the ketchup, tamarind paste, tomato paste, Worcestershire sauce, Tabasco, honey, vinegar, and pepper over medium heat. Cook just long enough to form a glossy, mahogany-colored glaze, about 7 minutes.

12. Brush a thin layer of the glaze over the top and sides of the meatloaf. Return it to the oven and broil for 2 to 3 minutes. Brush it again with more glaze and broil for 3 to 4 minutes more, until the meatloaf has turned a deep, burnished brown.

13. Let it rest for 15 minutes before serving. Garnish with more parsley.

Glaze
(Makes a generous ½ cup)

¼ cup ketchup

2 tablespoons tamarind paste

1½ teaspoons tomato paste

½ teaspoon Worcestershire sauce

1 teaspoon Tabasco or other mild hot sauce

1½ teaspoons honey

2 tablespoons distilled white vinegar

¼ teaspoon freshly ground black pepper

TAMARIND ROAST CHICKEN

I love the combination of tamarind with chicken: the way it deepens the color of the skin, scents the flesh, and gives it an unmistakable puckery tang. I recommend serving with Crispy Coconut Rice (page 132) and Hibiscus Baked Beans (page 135). Pull any leftover meat from the bones and refrigerate it in an airtight container, for other recipes. Reserve the bones for stock by simply freezing them in a zip-top bag.

SERVES 6

- 1 (5-pound) whole chicken, giblets packet removed
- 5½ teaspoons kosher or coarse sea salt (use 1 teaspoon per pound of chicken), divided
- 1 pound small red potatoes, scrubbed well
- 1 medium red onion, cut into quarters
- 2 oranges, cut into quarters
- 1 very ripe plantain, whole with the skin on
- 1 small garlic head, top cut off (to expose the cloves)
- 2 tablespoons tamarind paste
- 8 tablespoons (1 stick) salted butter, at room temperature

1. Thoroughly pat dry the chicken, inside and out, with paper towels, then rub it all over with the 5 teaspoons salt, including the cavity (or ½ teaspoon of fine sea salt or iodized salt per pound). Place the bird on a small-rimmed baking sheet, breast side up, and refrigerate, uncovered, for at least 1 hour and preferably overnight. (The skin will dry and tighten.)

2. Preheat the oven to 425°F.

3. In a roasting pan, spread the potatoes, onion, oranges, plantain, and garlic and season with the remaining ½ teaspoon salt. Remove the chilled chicken from the fridge, pat dry again, then set the chilled chicken over the produce, breast side up.

4. In a medium bowl, stir together the tamarind paste and butter, then use all of that mixture to coat the chicken inside and out, including gently loosening the breast skin to work it in underneath as well.

5. Cover with aluminum foil and roast for 30 minutes. Remove the foil and baste with the pan juices. Roast for an additional 30 to 40 minutes, until an instant-read thermometer inserted into the breast meat registers 160°F and the thigh meat registers 165°F. The potatoes and onion will be quite tender and the chicken will be darkened in spots and golden brown all over. Transfer the bird from the pan to a cutting board or serving platter to rest for at least 10 minutes before carving.

6. Stir the roasted vegetables in the pan to coat them with any pan juices, and serve with the roasted chicken.

MALTA-BRAISED SHORT RIBS

Malta was my mother's go-to drink. It's a nonalcoholic carbonated beverage that's very thick, very dark, and very sweet. It tastes of toasted barley and molasses. It's not something you find often outside of a Latin grocery store, and if by the grace of God my mother stumbled upon it at a neighborhood supermarket, she'd immediately put two six-packs in the cart. As soon as we got home and the groceries were put away, she took a dark brown bottle, divided its syrupy content between two glasses and once the fizz had died down, added ice and poured in milk. She handed me a glass and sipped hers while she smoked and thumbed through magazines. To this day if I see bottles of it in a store, I feel welcome.

Adding malta to a braise is almost like adding Coke, except the sauce becomes earthier, darker, with just a touch of sweetness. For me this dish is weeknight fancy at its best. Pressure cooking short ribs ensures tender fall-off-the-bone results in under an hour. Quick pickled peppers are a vibrant and punchy garnish that cuts through the fattiness of the ribs. Serve with Crispy Coconut Rice (page 132) or a simple mashed yuca.

If there are leftovers, they'll taste even better the next day, after the flavors in the sauce develop and deepen. Cover the meat in the sauce and store in an airtight container. Refrigerate up to three days or freeze for up to two months. Pickled peppers will remain fresh refrigerated in an airtight container for up to two months.

SERVES 4

Short Ribs

2 tablespoons canola oil, plus more as needed

1½ teaspoons Sazón (page 33)

8 bone-in beef short ribs (4 to 5 pounds total)

Kosher salt

1½ cups Recaíto (page 34)

½ cup chicken stock or broth

1 tablespoon tomato paste

1 tablespoon distilled white vinegar

1 teaspoon dried oregano

2 bay leaves

1½ cups red wine

12 to 14 ounces malta

1 tablespoon unsalted butter

Freshly ground black pepper

3 tablespoons fresh, chopped scallion, for garnish

Pickled Peppers

¼ cup distilled white vinegar

1 teaspoon honey

1 garlic clove

Pinch of salt

3 small sweet peppers

1. Make the Short Ribs: Combine the oil and Sazón in your electric pressure cooker then set it on HIGH.

2. Use paper towels to pat dry the short ribs. Season them with a generous amount of salt. Working in batches as needed, sear the short ribs for about 4 minutes per side, or until browned all over; note that they will not be cooked through. Transfer to a plate

3. Add the Recaíto to the pot and cook for 6 to 8 minutes, until it is fragrant, bubbling, and begins to darken. Use a wooden spoon to dislodge any browned bits.

4. Carefully pour in the stock. Add the tomato paste, vinegar, oregano, and bay leaves. Add all of the red wine and enough of the malta so the ribs will be covered.

5. Return all the ribs to the pot, placing them bone side up so the meat is submerged. Seal, set on HIGH PRESSURE, and cook for 45 minutes. When that cook time is up, allow the pressure to dissipate with a natural release.

Continues

6. Carefully open the pot and use tongs to transfer the ribs to a deep platter. The rib meat should fall off the bone. Discard the bones and cut away/discard any rubbery sinew from the ribs.

7. Using a fine-mesh strainer, strain the remaining liquid in the pressure cooker into a medium saucepan over medium heat, discarding the solids. Simmer for 35 to 40 minutes, until the liquid is reduced by half and its consistency is syrupy.

8. Remove from the heat and whisk in the butter until melted, which should thicken the liquid further and make it glossy. Taste, and adjust the seasoning with salt and pepper as needed. Pour over the ribs.

9. Make the pickled peppers: Combine the vinegar, ¼ cup water, the honey, garlic, and the pinch of salt in a small, microwave-safe glass jar. Microwave until boiling, about 1½ minutes. Stir to ensure the honey and salt have dissolved.

10. Using a Mandoline, cut the peppers as thinly as possible (about an ⅛ inch thick; you should have ½ cup) and add them to the jar, which should be filled to the top. Cool completely, for about thirty minutes, and then seal with a lid. If you don't have a mandolin, use a very sharp knife to create ⅛-inch-thick slices.

11. To serve, scatter the pickled peppers over the ribs as a tangy garnish. Finish with scallions.

MUSHROOM PASTELÓN

Pastelón is my favorite Puerto Rican dish. It's my go-to when I'm celebrating and my go-to when I'm trying to put the pieces back together. Think of it as a lasagna of sorts, but instead of pasta sheets, it's layered with tangy slices of sweet plantain. My Abuela Dora made it for special occasions with loads of *picadillo*, a savory beef mix with raisins and alcaparrado. I've made this vegetarian version dozens of times, and it's just as good as the meat-based one.

To lighten the workload, you can make the mushroom mixture the day before and refrigerate it in an airtight container. It's always nice to give the flavors time to mingle and deepen. Then all you need to do is assemble the *pastelón* and bake the next day. This dish is traditionally served with rice and beans.

SERVES 8

- 1 tablespoon plus 1½ teaspoons olive oil
- 1½ cups Recaíto (page 34)
- ½ teaspoon dried oregano
- ½ teaspoon Sazón (page 33)
- 1 teaspoon kosher salt, plus more as needed
- ¼ teaspoon freshly ground black pepper
- 1 pound mixed mushrooms (such as oyster, shiitake, and/or cremini) trimmed and chopped
- 1 cup frozen/defrosted cut green beans (2-inch pieces)
- ½ cup alcaparrado, olives cut crosswise into thin slices
- ½ cup dark raisins
- 1 tablespoon dry sherry (may substitute a dry Sauvignon Blanc or Pinot Grigio)
- 1½ teaspoons distilled white vinegar
- ¾ cup plain tomato sauce
- Cooking oil spray
- 1½ pounds frozen whole sweet plantains, cut in half then lengthwise into ¼-inch-thick slices
- 3 large eggs, lightly beaten
- 3 cups shredded mozzarella cheese
- ¼ cup freshly grated Parmigiano-Reggiano cheese

1. Preheat the oven to 400°F.

2. In a large heavy pot, heat the olive oil over medium heat until it shimmers. Stir in the Recaíto and cook for about 5 minutes, or until it has thickened.

3. Add the oregano, Sazón, salt, and pepper, stirring to incorporate. Once heated through, add the mushrooms and cook, stirring a few times, for about 8 minutes, or until the mushrooms have released their liquid and darkened in color.

4. Add the green beans, alcaparrado, raisins, sherry, vinegar, and tomato sauce, stirring to incorporate. Taste, and add more salt as needed. Reduce the heat to medium-low and cook for about 8 minutes, or until the mixture is bubbling and slightly thickened.

5. Lightly grease a deep lasagna pan with cooking oil spray. Use a third of the sliced plantains to line the bottom of the pan. Top with half the mushroom/green bean mixture. Drizzle with half of the beaten eggs. Top with 1 cup mozzarella. Repeat this layering process a second time.

6. Top with the remaining plantains, the remaining 1 cup mozzarella, and the Parmigiano-Reggiano. Bake for about 30 minutes, or until the cheese has melted and lightly browned, and the pastelón is bubbling at the edges. Let it cool for about 10 minutes before serving.

GUAVA-GLAZED PORK CHOPS

My abuela made pork chops every other day: pan-fried and served with a side of rice and beans. It wasn't until many years later that I had a pork chop with apple slices. It seemed like a preposterous pairing . . . until my first bite! This is a spin on that classic dish, with a buttery and acidic guava sauce. I suggest serving with my Roasted Green Papaya and Carrots (page 136).

SERVES 2

- 2 (8-ounce) bone-in pork chops, about 1 inch thick
- 2 teaspoons kosher salt
- 2 tablespoons canola oil
- 1 small yellow onion, sliced into ¼-inch-thick half-moons
- ¼ teaspoon Sazón (page 33)
- ¼ teaspoon Adobo (page 30)
- 3 whole guavas, frozen/defrosted and cut into ½-inch-thick slices
- 1 bay leaf
- ¾ cup chicken stock or broth
- 1 tablespoon tomato paste
- 1 tablespoon distilled white vinegar
- 2 tablespoons salted butter
- 1 tablespoon fresh lemon juice
- ¼ cup crumbled queso fresco, for garnish
- 1 tablespoon cilantro leaves, finely chopped, for garnish

1. Set an ovenproof rack inside a rimmed baking sheet lined with aluminum foil. Use paper towels to pat dry the pork chops. Season them with the salt (1 teaspoon per chop) and place them on the rack. Refrigerate, uncovered, for at least 1 hour, and preferably overnight.

2. In a 12-inch skillet, heat the oil over medium-high heat until it shimmers. Add the pork chops, turning to sear them on each side, including the fat sides and ends. They should be golden brown all over. Cook for a total of 10 to 12 minutes, turning them as needed, to an internal temperature of 145°F on an instant-read thermometer. Meanwhile, clean the rack you used for them so it can serve as a place to rest the cooked chops.

3. Remove the chops to the rack, and drain off/discard all but 2 tablespoons of rendered fat from the pan. Add the onion, Sazón, and Adobo to the pan and cook for about 2 minutes, until the onions have wilted and taken on a light yellow color. Add the guavas to the pan, along with the bay leaf, stock, tomato paste, and vinegar. Using a wooden spoon, stir to dislodge any browned bits. Cook the guava slices and onion for about another 3 minutes, or until a loose sauce forms.

4. Reduce the heat to medium or medium-low. Continue to cook the remaining liquid in the pan for about 5 minutes, or until it thickens enough to coat the back of a spoon. Remove from the heat; discard the bay leaf. Stir in the butter and lemon juice; cook for 1 to 2 minutes, until the butter has melted and the sauce becomes glossy.

5. To serve, dress the pork chops with the pan sauce. Scatter the cheese and cilantro on top.

JACKFRUIT ROPA VIEJA

I spent most of my high school years on the island and my favorite school lunch (besides frituras) was *ropa vieja*. The lunch ladies stared blankly as they scooped this glorious stewed meat on a bed of white rice and shoved it into my welcoming hands. It didn't matter that the girls in my sophomore class spent most of the morning making fun of me because I had to take my Spanish class with third graders. I could get lost in that ropa vieja and its unctious tangy broth. This is my vegan version. Serve it over Crispy Coconut Rice (page 132) or with slices of crusty bread. I love using yuca bread, which is crunchy and gluten-free.

SERVES 6

- 2 tablespoons olive oil
- 1 medium onion, cut into ¼-inch-thick half-moons
- 1 red bell pepper, stemmed, seeded, and cut into strips (about 2 x ¼-inch thick)
- 6 large garlic cloves, minced
- 1 tablespoon tomato paste
- ½ cup Recaíto (page 34)
- 2 cups plain tomato sauce
- 1 teaspoon soy sauce
- 1½ teaspoons Sazón (page 33)
- 1 (20-ounce) can green jackfruit, drained and coarsely chopped
- 1½ cups low-sodium vegetable broth
- 1 bay leaf
- ½ cup sliced, pimento-stuffed Manzanilla olives
- ¼ cup chopped cilantro, for garnish

1. In a large heavy skillet, heat the olive oil over medium-high heat until it shimmers. Stir in the onion and bell pepper; cook for about 2 minutes, or just until the onion is translucent and the bell pepper has softened.

2. Add the garlic and cook for about 30 seconds, or until fragrant, then stir in the tomato paste and the Recaíto. Cook for about 5 minutes, or until the mixture thickens.

3. Add the tomato sauce, soy sauce, Sazón, and jackfruit and cook for about 5 minutes, or until the mixture has thickened further and deepened in color.

4. Add the broth, bay leaf, and olives. Reduce the heat to medium-low, cover, and cook for 30 minutes, stirring occasionally to prevent the jackfruit from sticking. Then uncover and cook for 10 minutes more, so the liquid reduces and the mixture thickens a bit. Discard the bay leaf.

5. Plate and garnish with the cilantro.

Part Three

A Puerto Rican Le Speak S

arns to
panglish

It doesn't matter what room I'm in, I never feel like I quite fit in. I've always felt this way. I spent most of my childhood moving from place to place, never really having the time to build strong friendships. I attended twenty-three different schools before I hit high school. I didn't go to college, but instead worked at restaurants surrounded by people that also felt like outsiders in the rooms they were in. We were a gang of odds and ends, but when we made a restaurant sing on a Saturday night, we briefly belonged to one another.

But I needed more than that brief bit of belonging. I needed a purpose in my life, a career. So when I was twenty-four years old, I signed up for broadcasting school. It was a six-week course. On Day 1, my instructor asked what my dream was, and I said I wanted to tell food stories and host a show on Food Network, just like Emeril. On my way to school on Day 3, my car got T-boned by a dump truck.

I woke up from a coma to find that I had nineteen broken ribs, cracked bones in my neck, and a punctured lung. I checked myself out of the hospital as soon as I could stand and finished the last three weeks of school, picking broken glass from my scalp and popping Aleve like M&M's.

In the twelve years that followed, I forgot about food stories and became a radio host. I started a career in stand-up comedy. In the process, I moved across state lines seven times. I fell in love. I got married and had a son. I built a beautiful life for myself.

And then, well, things went topsy-turvy. I got divorced. I quit comedy and radio. I spent my savings nursing my two-year-old back to health from an almost lethal bout with MRSA (a staph bacterial infection). My best friend was murdered in cold blood, and I couldn't afford to go to his funeral in Florida. I found myself in the darkest depression of my life. I was an unemployed, broke, single mom, and I was scared to death.

Somewhere in the fog that followed, I remembered my dream of telling food stories. I thought, *It's too late. I'm too old.* And then the true blessing of hitting rock bottom revealed itself: I had nothing left to lose.

When I got the opportunity to audition for Gordon Ramsay on *MasterChef*, I was thirty-six years old, freshly divorced, and unemployed. I had no money, and nothing to my name left to sell. I was facing homelessness with a two-year-old. I found myself in the ludicrous position where trying to win a world-renowned cooking competition was the only way I was going to keep my kid and me off the streets of LA. I had no formal culinary training and no way to afford it, so I did what I had to do and taught myself. The producers asked me to put myself on a plate, to define my cuisine, but I didn't know how.

It was hard to see myself in a singular space. Of course the flavors of Puerto Rico, like sofrito, plantain, and picadillo felt like home. But so did continental American favorites, from Sloppy Joes to biscuits and gravy. If my kitchen could talk, it would speak Spanglish.

If I'm going to put myself on a plate, I must approach it the way I've lived, walking between two worlds, borrowing the best from each, never fully belonging to one or the other. But first, I needed to teach myself the basics.

I spent almost three months cooking nonstop in a tiny 400-square-foot studio apartment. I took care of my toddler during the day, and read borrowed cookbooks at night while he slept. I was on a $10-a-day food budget. I couldn't afford the ingredients to practice advanced techniques, so I taught myself knife skills with Dollar Store veggies, which became soup the next day. I learned how to make dressings and sauces. I could afford flour and eggs, so I taught myself how to make pasta, quick breads, and every way you could make an egg. I didn't sleep more than a few hours a night for weeks and weeks on end.

On the day of my audition, I learned that the only way into the *MasterChef* kitchen was to get one of just eighteen aprons, slim chances considering my lack of experience and the skill level of the ninety-nine other hopefuls in the dirty warehouse we were cooking in.

I had no idea my elbows could tremble when I was scared enough. But when I finally got the chance to cook for Gordon, holy-ish was I scared enough. I couldn't afford a new outfit, so I auditioned in my old maternity clothes. I covered the holes in my shirt with an apron, the hole in my right shoe with duct tape. I felt less than, but I was determined.

One of the producers led me to the double doors that Gordon was sitting behind. As the doors opened, she smiled gently at me and said, "You can do this." And then all the air rushed out of my lungs, and I started to cry.

Because I didn't think I could.

I planned to make my Abuela Dora's *pastelón*, a Puerto Rican casserole of sorts consisting of a sweet and savory picadillo, loads of cheese, green beans, and layers of fried sweet yellow plantain. When my marriage fell apart, it was the dish that pulled me together and inspired me to visit my homeland. And now I hoped it would show Gordon who I am in one bite. A bite that could change my life.

The plantains the producers had sourced for me were not ripe enough to slice and fry, so I boiled them and mashed them with a little butter and brown sugar. I topped the picadillo with the mash the way you do a shepherd's pie, one of Gordon's favorite dishes. That pivot, from slices of plantain to mashed plantain, turns a *pastelón* into a *piñón*. Gordon tasted the piñón then stared at me for what felt like years. He furrowed his brows and said succinctly, "There's something to you." I had to hold on to the counter to keep my knees from buckling.

It's been over a decade, and I still can't watch the footage of Gordon handing me my *MasterChef* apron without crying. It was the moment that changed the trajectory of my entire life.

I wasn't the best cook in the *MasterChef* kitchen that year, by far. But I was determined to stay for as long as possible to collect the day rate producers gave us ($50 a day) and use it to pay my rent. I made it to the Top 5.

I didn't win the cookbook deal or the $250,000 prize money I desperately needed. But I did get my foot in the door. And when you're stubborn and hell-bent, sometimes that's all it takes. After leaving *MasterChef*, I devoured cookbooks and experimented in my home kitchen nonstop. I worked in restaurant kitchens two days a week for free so that I could learn more. To help make ends meet, I waitressed double shifts four days a week. I was on my feet so much I had to go up two shoe sizes to make room for the swelling.

Two years after *MasterChef*, I got to host a special on FYI called *Make My Food Famous*, where home cooks compete to get their dishes on their favorite restaurant's menu. I kept hustling. I started catering what I dubbed Cali-Rican cuisine: dishes that showed off Puerto Rico's flavors developed with California technique. I started working as a line cook.

Three years after *MasterChef*, I landed the opportunity to host a digital series about baby food for Jessica Alba's Honest Company. I asked the director if he needed help and landed my first scriptwriting and recipe development gig. I taught myself how to shoot and edit and started creating content. I started running a kitchen.

Four years after *MasterChef*, I got a call from Food Network. They wanted me to audition to host a show. I was in the middle of a waitressing shift. I felt so faint I had to sit on the floor. I had prepared for four years straight. I was ready, and I nailed it.

Since that day, I've shot shows for Roku, Netflix, PBS, and more. I've had the opportunity to demo my recipes at food festivals all over the country. I've worked with the James Beard Foundation, the Jacques Pépin Foundation, and The Trotter Project. I've written for *Bon Appetít, Spruce Eats,* and *The Washington Post*. And now, dear reader, there is this book that you've almost reached the end of.

I wouldn't be where I am today if my entire life hadn't fallen apart. It gave me the opportunity to make something from nothing.

Every lousy turn has a purpose. Every obstacle has a gift. Find the purpose. Find the gift.

I found the meaning of life on a cutting board. Who knows where you'll find yours?

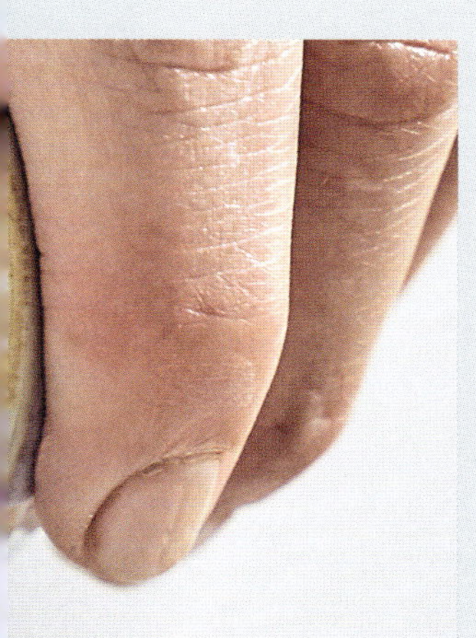

Things You Can Spill

Syrups, Sweet Sauces, and Spreads

ANNATTO, COCONUT, & DARK CHOCOLATE SYRUP

When my twin brother and I were very little, my Abuela Dora and Abuelo Quique would take us on a weekly shopping excursion to Woolworths. After my abuela had spent what felt like hours poring over fabrics and my abuelo had spent even more time tinkering in the tool section, we stopped at the cafeteria for a little pick-me-up. We always ended our lunches with a banana split, drenched in whipped cream, Maraschino cherries, and sweet chocolate syrup.

Making this Annatto, Coconut, and Dark Chocolate Syrup always takes me back to that cafeteria booth, where my thighs would stick to the vinyl, to when my twin brother and I still held each other's hands, and my grandparents were still in their prime. I could live in that moment forever.

Drizzle this syrup over fruit, ice cream, or mix it into my Malta Float (page 201). When choosing chocolate, steer clear of chocolate chips, which keep their shape at high heat. Instead, opt for dark chocolate in the 70 to 85 percent range. Likewise, you want to steer clear of milk chocolate, as combining it with the cream of coconut will leave you with cloyingly sweet results.

MAKES ABOUT 2¾ CUPS

1 cup well-shaken cream of coconut

1 tablespoon Annatto Oil (page 37)

Pinch of kosher salt

2 cups coarsely chopped dark chocolate (at least 70% cacao)

TIP: **To make clean up a breeze, chop the chocolate on a piece of parchment paper. This will also make it easier to add the chopped chocolate to the coconut mixture. A serrated knife works best for chopping chocolate.**

1. In a microwave-safe bowl, stir together the cream of coconut, Annatto Oil, and the pinch of salt. Microwave in 15-second increments until the mixture starts to steam and lightly bubble. The oil will separate on the surface; this is okay.

2. Stir in the chocolate and allow it to melt. There is no need to microwave it. Just let the mixture sit for about 2 minutes at room temperature, or until the chocolate has melted, then stir to form a smooth, shiny sauce.

3. Cool completely, then refrigerate in an airtight container for up to 2 months.

GUAVA CREAM CHEESE

In Puerto Rico, guava paste, or *pasta de guayaba*, is often served at the end of a meal, sliced and layered with queso fresco or fresh farmer's cheese. It's also popular in pastries paired with cream cheese, like the puff pastry-based *pastelillos de guayaba*. This cream cheese has the guava paste mixed into it, which helps it spread as easy as room temperature butter. I use it on toast, bagels, piped into strawberries, and as a glaze for a simple butter cake.

You can source guava paste at any Latin grocery store, where you'll find it in flat round cans or in plastic-wrapped blocks.

MAKES ABOUT 1½ CUPS

- 2 tablespoons water
- 2 tablespoons fresh lime juice
- ⅛ teaspoon ground ginger
- 4 ounces guava paste, cut into ½-inch dice (see Tip; about ½ cup)
- 1 cup cream cheese, at room temperature
- Pinch of kosher salt

TIP: **To keep the guava paste from sticking to the knife, grease a paper towel with a little oil and then rub it along both sides of the knife.**

1. In a small skillet or sauté pan, set over medium heat, stir together 2 tablespoons water, the lime juice, and ginger.

2. When bubbles form at the edges, reduce the heat to medium-low and add the guava paste. Use a flexible spatula to help break down the guava. Cook for a few minutes, stirring constantly, to form a smooth jam. You should be able to run the spatula across the bottom of the pan and have its path remain for at least 3 seconds. Cool completely.

3. In the bowl of a stand mixer fitted with a balloon-whisk attachment, beat the cream cheese on medium speed until creamy, stopping to scrape down the bowl once or twice. Add the cooled guava jam and the pinch of salt, then beat on medium-low speed until fully incorporated. The cream cheese will be a soft pink and the consistency of a spread. Refrigerate in an airtight container for up to 1 week.

GUANABANA QUICK JAM

In Puerto Rico, we call soursop *guanabana*. On the big continent, it might also be called a "custard apple." The fresh fruit looks like a ginormous green pear with tiny spiky bumps on its skin. The velvety pulp has delicate flavors: floral strawberry, tart green apple, and light citrus notes. It can be difficult to source fresh soursop. You might find some at a well-stocked Latin market. It's much easier to source frozen or as bottled pulp.

I love to make a quick jam from guanabana to spread on buttered toast, pancakes, or to star in my Guanabana Jam Pound Cake (page 182). You can also stir it into oatmeal, add it to milkshakes, and fold it into whipped cream. Store in an airtight container up to ten days in the fridge and up to three months in the freezer.

MAKES ABOUT 1 CUP

- 1¾ cups (14 ounces) fresh or frozen/defrosted soursop pulp
- 2 teaspoons fresh lime juice
- ¼ cup granulated sugar
- Pinch of kosher salt
- 1 tablespoon cornstarch
- ¼ cup water

1. If using fresh pulp, use a food processor or blender to puree the soursop pulp until creamy. Place a fine-mesh strainer over a heavy saucepan and use a spatula to push the puree through, discarding any solids left behind. Generally speaking, frozen or bottled pulp is already blended. You can place the pulp directly in the heavy saucepan and use a stick blender to smooth out any lumps.

2. Add the lime juice, sugar, and the pinch of salt. Place over medium heat and cook for 12 to 15 minutes, stirring occasionally to avoid scorching, until the soursop slightly deepens in color. The mixture should be creamy, bubbling, and thick enough to coat the back of a spoon.

3. Mix the cornstarch into the water then stir it into the bubbling guanabana. Allow to boil for 1 minute, stirring constantly, to completely incorporate the slurry. Let cool, then you can use the jam right away. Refrigerate in an airtight container for up to 10 days or freeze for up to 3 months.

TIPS: **If you luck out and find fresh soursop, you'll know it's ripe when you press its surface and it feels soft and spongy. To harvest fresh pulp, peel using a veggie peeler or a knife. Slice the fruit down the center and cut out the stringy heart. Use a spoon to remove the large black seeds.**

The cornstarch will thicken the guanabana into a velvety consistency. To activate the cornstarch's thickening powers, you must boil the quick jam for 1 minute.

MANGO SAUCE

Mangoes are my favorite fruit. The very word conjures up images of sunshine, warm breezes, and the vibrant spirit of my childhood home in Mayagüez, a town renowned for its ridiculously tasty mangoes. The scent of a perfectly ripe mango is pure nostalgia, transporting me back to lazy summer days spent devouring these juicy gems fresh from the tree.

This mango sauce recipe is a personal favorite, not only because it's incredibly easy to make, but because it can bring me back home in one sweet, tangy, bite. I mix it into oatmeal and serve it over bread pudding and rice pudding.

MAKES ABOUT 2 CUPS

1 heaping cup (about 5 ounces) frozen mango chunks

¼ cup granulated sugar

½ cup unsweetened mango juice (if sweetened, reduce the sugar to 2 tablespoons)

1½ teaspoons cornstarch

Pinch of ground ginger

1 lime

1. In a small heavy saucepan, over medium-high heat, combine the mango, sugar, and ¼ cup of the mango juice. Bring to a boil, stirring occasionally, and cook for several minutes, mashing the mango chunks to help break them down.

2. Use a vegetable peeler to zest the lime in long strips. Juice the lime, reserving ½ tablespoon for the recipe. The rest of the juice can be used for other preparations.

3. Meanwhile, in a small bowl, whisk together the cornstarch and the remaining mango juice to make a smooth slurry.

4. Add the slurry to the saucepan, stirring and cooking just long enough to form a sauce that coats the back of a spoon. Mix in the ginger, the ½ tablespoon lime juice, and lime zest. The soft, chunky sauce will thicken further as it cools. Refrigerate in an airtight container for about 2 weeks or freeze for up to 3 months.

DULCE DE LECHE WHIPPED CREAM

In the '80s, my mother had a habit of eating condensed milk straight from the can with a soup spoon as she watched her favorite American soap opera, *Guiding Light.* During commercial breaks, she yelled for me from the living room. It was my job to change the channels for her so she could see what else was on. (Kids were the first remote controls.)

I remember the first time I watched her boil a can of condensed milk on our electric stove top. Every half hour or so, she added water to replace what had evaporated from the small pot it was in. After much of the day was gone, she took the can out, let it cool, then used our rusty can opener to take off the top. Inside, the usually creamy white milk had thickened and darkened into what looked like peanut butter. I was hooked from the first moment I tasted *dulce de leche.*

In Puerto Rico, it's incorporated into desserts the same way you would caramel. Folding it into whipped cream cuts the sugariness considerably. Use this as a topping for pies, cheesecakes, pancakes, and waffles, and to garnish coffee drinks and milkshakes.

At the risk of upsetting every single one of my tías (aunties), please don't boil a can of condensed milk to make dulce de leche. Heating the can releases chemicals from the plastic lining. You can find it pre-made in most grocery stores. La Lechera is a great economical brand and the San Ignacio brand is pure magic.

MAKES ABOUT 4 CUPS

2 cups heavy whipping cream, well chilled

½ teaspoon vanilla extract

¼ cup confectioners' sugar

½ cup dulce de leche

Pinch of kosher salt

TIP: Add 3 pinches of kosher salt to make it a Salted Dulce de Leche Whipped Cream.

1. In the bowl of a stand mixer fitted with a balloon-whisk attachment or in a bowl using a handheld electric mixer, beat the heavy cream and vanilla on medium speed until soft peaks form.

2. Add the confectioners' sugar, a tablespoon at a time, and beat on medium-high speed until stiff peaks form.

3. Use a spatula to gently fold in the dulce de leche, until no white streaks remain.

4. Transfer to an airtight container and refrigerate for up to 3 days.

DARK RUM CARAMEL SAUCE

Rum-making is deeply rooted in Puerto Rican history. The Spanish colonizers set up sugarcane farms and rum factories all over the island. Many Boricuas worked the fields or the factories and, naturally, developed a love for the subtly sweet liquor. Puerto Rico is now considered the Rum Capital of the World. And while islanders drink loads of it, we also use it in our cooking.

This caramel sauce is creamy with a hint of smokiness and oak. Use it as a fruit dip, stirred into coffee, or drizzled over ice cream, bread pudding, and pies. Serve warm (although I like to eat a spoonful straight from the refrigerator).

MAKES ABOUT 1 CUP

4 tablespoons (½ stick) salted butter

½ (packed) cup light or dark brown sugar (see Tips)

⅓ cup heavy cream

2 tablespoons dark rum

¼ teaspoon vanilla extract

Pinch of salt

1. In a heavy saucepan, over medium-low heat, melt the butter until it foams and the milk solids turn a golden brown. Add the light brown sugar, whisking until it dissolves and a smooth caramel forms, about 3 to 4 minutes. Remove from the heat.

2. Whisk in the heavy cream until well blended, then add the rum, whisking until the caramel is a uniform color. Allow to cool for a few minutes, before stirring in the vanilla and salt.

3. Use right away, or cool completely and transfer to an airtight container. The sauce will thicken a bit as it cools. Store in an airtight container and keep at room temperature for up to 3 days, or refrigerate for up to 3 months.

TIPS: Use a heavy-bottomed saucepan with rounded sides. A straight-sided pan won't allow the whisk to reach the edges and will leave you with chunks of brown sugar.

Sift the brown sugar before adding it to the butter to ensure there are no rock-like clumps. Once you add the sugar to the butter it will be clumpy at first but will become smoother as it is heated. For best results, whisk continuously.

BANANA BUTTER-RUM SAUCE

This sauce is a warm hug on a cold day. Decadent and velvety, it pairs perfectly with my recipe for Pan de Bono Skillet Pancakes (page 56). I also love it over a simple scoop of vanilla ice cream or straight out of the jar. The bananas break up some as they cook, but still have a bit of texture. Make sure to use a good quality rum to add warmth and complexity.

I love making this with *guineos niños* (baby bananas), small, extra-sweet bananas often sold as "Lady Finger" bananas. I simply slice them in half lengthwise. You can also use regular bananas. Just cut them in half crosswise, then slice each piece into ¼-inch-thick planks.

MAKES ABOUT 2 CUPS

- 4 tablespoons (½ stick) salted butter
- 1 whole clove
- 1 whole star anise
- 2 bananas, cut in half lengthwise and then cut crosswise into slabs that are about ¼ inch thick
- ¼ (packed) cup light or dark brown sugar
- ¼ cup dark rum
- ½ teaspoon vanilla extract
- ¼ teaspoon ground cinnamon

1. In a medium skillet, over medium heat, combine the butter, clove, and star anise. Cook just until the butter has begun to foam and turn brown. Add the bananas and cook for 6 to 8 minutes, stirring gently, until they are lightly browned. Use a slotted spoon to transfer them to a plate.

2. Add the light brown sugar and rum to the pan. Cook for about 2 minutes, stirring until the sugar dissolves, the mixture is slightly syrupy, and the smell of alcohol has dissipated. Remove from the heat.

3. Add the vanilla and cinnamon, then slide the bananas back into the sauce, stirring to coat evenly. Store it in an airtight container and refrigerate for up to 2 weeks or freeze for up to 3 months.

PASSION FRUIT CURD

This custardy passion fruit spread is tart and tangy and impossible to stop eating, which is why I always make a double batch. Yes, you will be stirring a pot for close to twenty minutes. Yes, you will be ready to give up as it foams and refuses to thicken. Yes, you will wonder if this was a bigger waste of time than joining that overpriced dating site. (If you know, you know.) But once it magically starts to thicken and you take that first velvety bite, you'll see the trouble was worth it. Swirl it into a yogurt parfait or use it as a topper for Toasted Coconut Panna Cotta (page 189) or as the filling for Passion Fruit–Curd Mini Cakes (page 186). You can use fresh passion fruit, but it will cost $600,000 and you'll need to strain the seeds out of it. I use frozen passion fruit puree because it's economical and convenient. You can find it at most well-stocked grocery stores.

MAKES ABOUT 3½ CUPS

- 3 large eggs plus 3 large egg yolks, at room temperature
- 1 cup granulated sugar
- 1 cup unsweetened passion fruit puree
- 2 tablespoons fresh lime juice
- 8 tablespoons (1 stick) salted butter cut into chunks, at room temperature

1. Fill a large mixing bowl halfway with ice cubes and water. Set aside.

2. Place a medium saucepan half filled with water over medium heat, until it's barely bubbling at the edges.

3. In a heatproof bowl big enough to fit over the saucepan of water (without touching the water itself), whisk together the eggs and yolks, the sugar, passion fruit puree, and lime juice until well incorporated. Place the bowl on the pot and keep whisking for 15 to 20 minutes. The mixture will be frothy before it begins to thicken.

4. Once the mixture is thick enough to coat the back of a spoon, whisk in a few chunks of the butter at a time, until melted and well blended. Transfer the bowl to the ice-water bath. Continue to whisk for about 5 minutes more, or until thoroughly chilled.

5. Transfer the curd to a container; if the surface is foamy, you may wish to skim that off. If the curd is not completely smooth, you may wish to push it through a fine-mesh strainer, discarding any solids (such as bits of egg).

6. Place plastic wrap directly on the curd's surface and refrigerate for at least 2 hours, or until softly set. At this point, the curd is ready to serve, or it can be transferred to an airtight container and refrigerated for up to 2 weeks or frozen for up to 3 months.

Sweet Surrender

Cakes, Puddings, and Other Sweet Treats

MORIR SOÑANDO NO-BAKE CHEESECAKE

In Puerto Rico, we have a drink called *morir soñando* (to die dreaming). Originally from the Dominican Republic, it's a refreshing, cooling blend of orange juice and milk served with loads of ice. It's perfect for a hot island day. But as great as it is in liquid form, it's even better as a creamy no-bake cheesecake. The cream cheese is mixed with tangy sour cream and lightened with whipped cream. That makes it a perfect foundation for the citrusy punch of the orange marmalade.

If the crust sticks to the pie plate, wet a dish towel with hot water, and squeeze out the excess. Place the pie plate on top of the towel for a minute to warm the crust. It will loosen right up! You can make this icebox pie up to two days ahead or freeze it tightly wrapped in plastic for up to three months. If serving on a scorching hot summer day, it might be best to freeze it until it's time for it to hit the table.

SERVES 8
(MAKES 1 DEEP-DISH 9-INCH PIE)

- 1 orange
- 1 cup heavy whipping cream
- 1 bay leaf
- 2 cups (about 8 ounces) crumbled, plain butter cookies, such as Royal Dansk brand
- 3 tablespoons granulated sugar, divided
- 8 tablespoons (1 stick) salted butter, melted, plus 1 tablespoon chilled butter
- ½ cup sour cream
- 2 cups cream cheese, at room temperature
- ½ cup powdered sugar
- 1 teaspoon vanilla extract
- 1 cup orange marmalade, plus ¼ cup for garnish

1. Using a Microplane or the small-hole side of a box grater, zest the orange. Set the zested orange aside.

2. In a small saucepan, heat the heavy cream over medium heat until it is steaming. Remove from the heat and add the orange zest and the bay leaf. Steep for 10 minutes, then transfer to a container, cover, and chill in the freezer for 15 minutes.

3. Meanwhile, in a food processor, pulse the cookies until they are reduced to fine crumbs. Transfer to a medium bowl; add 2 tablespoons of the granulated sugar and the melted butter. Use your hands to work the mixture to a sand-like consistency.

4. Transfer the cookie crumb mixture to a greased 9-inch, deep-dish pie plate. Using the bottom of a measuring cup, firmly press the crumbs into the dish, working outward from the center and then up the sides. Transfer to the freezer.

5. Remove the chilled cream from the freezer and remove bay leaf from the chilled cream, then combine the cream and the remaining tablespoon of granulated sugar in the bowl of a stand mixer fitted with a balloon-whisk attachment or use a handheld electric mixer. Beat on low speed to incorporate, then gradually raise the speed to high, beating to form soft peaks. Transfer the flavored whipped cream to a separate bowl; you'll use the now-empty mixer bowl again, without the need to clean it.

6. Add the sour cream, cream cheese, powdered sugar, and vanilla. Beat on medium speed until smooth and thoroughly incorporated. By hand, fold in the flavored whipped cream.

7. Pour the batter into the prepared crust. Add the orange marmalade in dollops and use a butter knife to cut it through the batter to create swirls. Cover the surface directly with parchment paper and freeze for 1 hour.

8. Take the cheesecake out of the freezer, discard the parchment, and refrigerate until you are ready to serve. Thinly slice the zested orange into rounds. Remove the pith (the white tissue lining the rind) by peeling it off gently, or using a pairing knife to cut around it. Top the cheesecake with a thin layer of the remaining marmalade and add the citrus rounds just before serving.

SPICED SWEET PLANTAIN PUDDING

If you cut me, I would probably bleed *plátanos maduros*. That's how much I love sweet plantain. These are ripened plantains whose once green skins have morphed from green to yellow and black. On the island, they are sliced and fried and served at breakfast, lunch, and dinner. Their sweet tangy flesh pairs well with eggs, or rice and beans, or layered in Mushroom Pastelón (page 149). I love them the most as a dessert.

Someone may look at a batch of plátanos maduros surrounded by fruit flies, grimace, and think, *Those need to be thrown out.* A Puerto Rican, however, will take one look and their mouth will begin to water. We know that though that plantain looks like it's been through hell and back, like it has nothing left to give, it is in fact a treasure at its peak of sweetness. Its best is still to come. *It's one of us.*

SERVES 4 (MAKES ABOUT 4 CUPS)

- 3 cups whole milk
- 1 cup heavy whipping cream
- 4 (3-inch) cinnamon sticks
- 2 whole cloves
- 1 whole vanilla bean, split lengthwise
- 1½ pounds frozen/defrosted prebaked plantains, roughly chopped
- ¼ cup granulated sugar
- ⅓ cup cornstarch
- ½ teaspoon kosher salt
- 10 large egg yolks (reserve the whites for a different preparation)
- 2 teaspoons cacao nibs, for garnish

1. In a deep saucepan, over medium heat, combine the milk, heavy cream, cinnamon sticks, cloves, vanilla bean, and plantains. Stirring occasionally, cook for about 8 minutes, or until the milk starts to steam and is barely bubbling at the edges. Remove from the heat, cover, and steep the plantains until the pot has cooled and the liquid is at room temperature. Cover and refrigerate for at least 6 hours, and preferably overnight.

2. Uncover the chilled saucepan; discard the cloves and cinnamon sticks. Return the saucepan to medium heat, stirring occasionally, until the mixture again is barely bubbling at the edges. Using a fine-mesh strainer set over a bowl and a flexible spatula, push the mixture through; the solids can be reserved for later use. Scrape the vanilla bean seeds into the strained liquid. (Plantain pulp can be used in pancakes; the scraped vanilla pod can be used to flavor sugar.)

3. Pour the mixture back into the saucepan and place over low heat. While the saucepan is still cool, whisk in the sugar, cornstarch, and salt until thoroughly incorporated. Whisk in the egg yolks and raise the heat to medium-low. Keep whisking; the mixture will steam and begin to thicken.

4. As soon as the surface bubbles disappear and the custard begins to become glossy, set a timer and continue to cook for 1 minute, whisking to form a thickened pudding. Remove from the heat.

5. Using the fine-mesh strainer and flexible spatula again, push the pudding through into a clean bowl, discarding any remaining solids (such as bits of cooked egg).

6. Divide among individual dessert dishes and serve hot. Can be garnished simply with cocoa nibs. Or go over the top and layer it with butter cookies and slices of sweet fried plantain. Leftovers can be refrigerated for up to 3 days. Do not reheat.

GUANABANA JAM POUND CAKE

My Abuela Dora loved Sara Lee Pound Cake. She kept a box of it jammed in our tiny fridge, between tubs of Imperial margarine that were so full of leftovers, their lids looked like tight belts on fat men. My abuela was not a woman of many words or many vices. But that slice of pound cake came out like clockwork once a day, a treat she would eat slowly and silently with her afternoon *cafecito* (coffee) after she had finished the ironing.

Her arthritic hands had a tough time opening and closing the aluminum container of the poundcake. It was my job to pick at the sharp crinkled silver edges, pushing them up when we wanted access, and squeezing them down when it was time to put the cake away again. This recipe was inspired by her, and every time I have a bite, I get a little choked up remembering those precious moments spent by her side. Moments that, at that time, I thought would never end.

SERVES 8 (MAKES ONE 8 X 4-INCH LOAF)

Cake

16 tablespoons (2 sticks) salted butter, at room temperature, plus more for greasing the pan

1½ cups all-purpose flour, plus more for the pan

½ teaspoon baking powder

¼ teaspoon baking soda

¼ teaspoon kosher salt

¾ cup granulated sugar

1 tablespoon light or dark brown sugar

4 large eggs, lightly beaten

¼ cup sour cream

¾ cup Guanabana Quick Jam (page 166), divided

Finely grated zest of 1 lime

Glaze

2 tablespoons whole milk

1 tablespoon powdered sugar

1. Preheat the oven to 350°F, and position a rack in the center of the oven.

2. Grease an 8½ x 4½-inch loaf pan with a little butter. Line the pan with parchment paper so that two sides overhang (to make extracting the baked cake easier), then grease the parchment with butter.

3. **Make the cake:** In a medium bowl, whisk together the flour, baking powder, baking soda, and salt.

4. In the bowl of a stand mixer or using a handheld electric mixer, combine the butter, granulated sugar, and light brown sugar. Beat on medium speed for several minutes, or until light and fluffy. Stop to scrape down the bowl.

5. Add the eggs, sour cream, a ½ cup of the Guanabana Quick Jam, and half the lime zest. Beat on low speed until well incorporated. Stop to scrape down the bowl again, then add half the flour mixture, and combine until incorporated, beating on low speed to form a smooth batter. Then add the remaining flour mixture.

6. Transfer to the prepared loaf pan, spreading the surface evenly into the corners. Bake for 45 to 50 minutes, until the top of the cake springs back when you press it with a finger, and a toothpick inserted into the center comes out clean.

7. Cool in the pan for 10 minutes, then dislodge by lifting it out using the parchment overhang. Transfer to a cooling rack set over a sheet of wax paper, discarding the parchment.

8. **Make the glaze:** In a small bowl, mix the remaining ¼ cup of Guanabana Quick Jam with the milk and powdered sugar until smooth. Drizzle over the warm pound cake. Sprinkle the remaining lime zest over the top and serve.

MALTA & CHOCOLATE BUNDT CAKE

There's not much that I love more than chocolate cake. It wasn't something I tasted growing up on a small defunct dairy farm in Boquerón, Puerto Rico. I had my first life-changing bite at my elementary school in Houston, Texas. It was a small square of dry chocolate sheet cake with crackled chocolate frosting. I inhaled it, licking the frosting off my fingers, thankful my mother couldn't see me picking up crumbs off the table. At least I was cleaning up after myself, I reasoned. I truly believe there is a chocolate cake for every occasion, and this one is a Sunday afternoon cake. The kind that gives you the stamina you need to face a Monday (mostly because there should be a few slices left over for you to devour then). It's moist, thanks to the addition of sour cream, with loads of caramel notes thanks to the malta.

SERVES 12

Cake

16 tablespoons (2 sticks) salted butter, plus more, for greasing the pan

½ cup unsweetened cocoa powder, sifted

2 cups all-purpose flour, plus more for the pan

2 (packed) cups light brown sugar

½ teaspoon kosher salt

2 teaspoons baking powder

1 cup malta, at room temperature

½ cup full-fat or low-fat sour cream

2 large eggs

1 teaspoon vanilla extract

Glaze

8 tablespoons (1 stick) salted butter

2 tablespoons heavy cream

¼ cup unsweetened cocoa powder, sifted

1 cup confectioners' sugar, sifted

½ teaspoon vanilla extract

¼ cup unsweetened flaked coconut, for garnish

1. Preheat the oven to 350°F, and position a rack in the center of the oven.

2. Make the cake: In a small saucepan over medium heat, melt the butter. Allow it to foam, swirling the pan occasionally so the butter browns but does not burn. Remove from the heat and stir in the cocoa powder until fully incorporated.

3. While the butter browns, grease a 12-cup Bundt pan generously with butter. Add enough flour to thoroughly coat the pan, shaking off any excess. Place the coated pan in the freezer.

4. In a mixing bowl, whisk together the flour, brown sugar, salt, and baking powder.

5. In a large liquid measuring cup, stir the malta, sour cream, eggs, and vanilla until well blended. Add a few tablespoons of the chocolate mixture to temper the egg mixture until it's warm, then stir in the remaining chocolate mixture.

6. Pour the chocolate mixture into the mixing bowl with the flour mixture and stir until no trace of dry ingredients remains. The batter should be shiny, smooth, and thick.

7. Pour the batter evenly into the prepared frozen Bundt pan and bake 35 to 42 minutes or until the cake springs back when you press a finger on its surface. The edges should pull from the pan and a toothpick inserted in the thickest area should come out clean. Cool on a rack to room temperature.

8. Once the cake has cooled, make the glaze: In a large saucepan over medium heat, combine the butter, heavy cream, cocoa powder, and confectioners' sugar. Cook, stirring, for a few minutes, until bubbly, the sugar has dissolved, and the glaze is smooth and glossy. Remove from the heat and stir in the vanilla.

9. Remove the cooled cake from its pan and place on a platter. Drizzle the warm glaze over the top. Garnish with the flaked coconut.

TIP: If you do not have a 12-cup Bundt pan, use a 10 x 2-inch round cake pan or a 9 x 9-inch square cake pan.

PASSION FRUIT–CURD MINI CAKES

I tried a Twinkie for the first time when I was twelve years old, and it was not love at first bite. The cake was strangely sticky to the touch and the filling was too sweet and smelled faintly of chemicals.

Twenty-five years later, I worked as a pastry chef at a now defunct dessert shop in LA, where I made traditional Twinkies with marshmallow filling from scratch every day. That's where I truly fell in love with their delightful shape, their light-as-air bite, and with the way they plump as you fill them.

You can buy a Twinkie baking pan online for about $15, but you don't need one to enjoy this recipe. If using a Twinkie pan, the batter will fill it all the way to the top. The Twinkies will fall out of their molds once baked. I then cut the overhang off with a bread knife to level the Twinkies, and keep the tops as chef snacks. If you don't have a Twinkie pan, use a standard muffin pan and raise the bake time by a few minutes or use a mini muffin pan and reduce the bake time by a few minutes. No matter what, it's still going to be delicious!

Steeping the annatto seeds in butter and milk gives the batter a beautiful deeply golden hue.

While I love these cakes paired with Passion Fruit Curd as the filling, you also can try using a half portion of Guava Cream Cheese (page 165).

MAKES 12 MINI CAKES

- 4 tablespoons (½ stick) salted butter
- 2 tablespoons annatto seeds
- ¾ cup pastry flour
- 1 tablespoon milk powder
- 1 teaspoon baking powder
- ¼ teaspoon kosher salt
- 16 tablespoons granulated sugar, divided
- 5 large eggs, separated into whites and yolks, at room temperature
- 2 tablespoons full-fat or low-fat milk
- ¼ cup sour cream
- ½ teaspoon vanilla extract
- Cooking spray
- ½ recipe Passion Fruit Curd (page 175)

TIP: **If you don't have annatto seeds, steep a 2 x 4-inch strip of orange zest in the cream and butter mixture and add a pinch of turmeric.**

1. Preheat the oven to 350°F, and position a rack in the center of the oven.
2. In a small microwave-safe bowl, melt the butter in 30-second increments until it foams then begins to turn light golden brown, about 1 minute 30 seconds to 2 minutes. Combine the butter and annatto seeds, and let steep for 15 minutes.
3. Meanwhile, in a small bowl, stir together the pastry flour, milk powder, baking powder, salt, and 2 tablespoons of the sugar.
4. In a mixing bowl, use a handheld electric mixer or a stand mixer fitted with whisk attachments on medium speed to beat the egg whites until frothy.
5. Gradually add 6 tablespoons of sugar to the egg whites, continuing to beat until soft glossy peaks form.
6. Clean the whisk attachment (no matter which mixer you use). Then, in a separate large bowl, use the mixer to beat the egg yolks with the remaining 8 tablespoons of sugar for about 5 minutes, or until they are pale yellow and lightened in texture.
7. Using a fine-mesh strainer, strain the steeping mixture, discarding the annatto seeds. Add that liquid to the buttery yellow egg yolk mixture along with the milk, sour cream, and vanilla, gently folding them in to create a batter.

Continues

8. Add the beaten egg whites to the beaten yolks and sprinkle in the flour mixture, folding gently to incorporate.

9. Using cooking spray, grease your Twinkie molds. Spoon enough batter into each mold to fill about a half inch from the top. Bake for 12 to 16 minutes, until the cakes are golden, and a toothpick inserted in the center of each one comes out clean. Cool completely.

10. If necessary, use a serrated knife to level the tops of each Twinkie. Invert them over so their flat sides are facing up. Use a chopstick to poke three equally spaced holes in the flat sides, being careful not to go through to the other side.

11. Fill a pastry bag with your Passion Fruit Curd, then use it to fill the holes in each Twinkie, being careful not to overstuff them. Store the Twinkies in the fridge in an airtight container for up to 5 days.

TOASTED COCONUT PANNA COTTA

This is my go-to party dessert. It is a light and subtly sweet finish to any meal. It can be made ahead and it travels well. When preparing, make sure to choose cream of coconut, which is sweetened, and not coconut cream. The cream of coconut should be stored in the fridge for about twenty minutes, which will help the waxy solids rise and separate from the sweetened cream of coconut. Then simply open the can from the bottom and use the liquid. The coconut cream solids can be reserved for another use.

SERVES 8

- 1 (15-ounce) can cream of coconut, refrigerated
- 2 cups heavy whipping cream
- 1½ cups whole milk
- 2 cups unsweetened toasted flaked coconut, plus 2 tablespoons for garnish
- 1 whole vanilla bean, split lengthwise
- 1 whole star anise
- ⅛ teaspoon freshly grated nutmeg
- ¼ cup cold water
- 3¾ teaspoons unflavored powdered gelatin
- Passion Fruit Curd (page 175) or Annatto, Coconut, and Dark Chocolate Syrup (page 162) (optional, for serving)

1. Open the can of cream of coconut from the bottom and pour the liquid into a heavy saucepan. Reserve the solidified coconut cream from the top of the can for another use. Add the heavy cream and milk to the saucepan. (If any further bits of solidified cream float to the surface, just skim them off to ensure a silky texture for the panna cotta.)

2. Add the flaked coconut, vanilla bean, star anise, and nutmeg. Cook over medium-low heat just until barely bubbling at the edges then remove from the heat.

3. Take out the vanilla bean and, using a knife, scrape its seeds into the pan then toss in the pod. Cover with a lid and steep the custard for 30 minutes.

4. When ready to assemble the panna cottas, arrange your small glass dishes or ramekins on a paper towel-lined tray. (I divide the mixture among eight 1-cup ramekins, but feel free to use whatever vessels you have on hand. Size isn't important.) Prepare an ice-water bath in a large bowl.

5. In a small bowl, pour in the cold water and sprinkle the powdered gelatin over the surface; let it sit for a few minutes to dissolve and firm up.

6. Place a fine-mesh strainer lined with cheesecloth over a bowl, pass the cooled cream mixture through, pressing the solids to extract all their liquid, then discard them. Return the mixture to its pot and warm through over medium heat, until barely bubbling at the edges and lightly steaming. Remove from the heat.

7. Whisk in the bloomed gelatin until completely dissolved. (You should no longer see any bits of gelatin on your whisk.) Pour this custard mixture back into the bowl and place the bowl in your ice-water bath. Cool for 20 minutes, then skim off any remaining solids, as needed, and strain again.

8. Divide the mixture evenly among the dishes or ramekins, being careful not to splash or spill on the outsides and rims. Cover them all with a single sheet of plastic wrap and refrigerate for at least 6 hours, preferably overnight.

9. Serve as is, or top with a dollop of Passion Fruit Curd or Annatto, Coconut, and Dark Chocolate Syrup.

TIP: If you can't source unsweetened toasted coconut flakes, you can toast unsweetened flakes yourself in a 325°F oven. Spread the coconut flakes in a thin layer on a rimmed baking sheet lined with parchment paper. Bake for about 3 minutes, then stir to expose more untoasted flakes. Bake for another 1 to 2 minutes, or until evenly, lightly browned.

PAN DE MALLORCA BACON CINNAMON ROLLS

I first encountered cinnamon rolls at my Houston elementary school breakfast. They reminded me of *mallorcas*, the snail-shaped pastries my abuelo often ate for breakfast—except these were loaded with fiery cinnamon and the creamiest sugary glaze. They were an oddity to me but a delicious one, nonetheless.

Mallorcas are plump, pillowy, buttery, Puerto Rican sweet rolls dusted with confectioners' sugar and often enjoyed for breakfast. They're GIANT. Sometimes, they are split down the center and used as buns for breakfast sandwiches.

I like to make the dough a day ahead so that assembly of the cinnamon rolls goes quickly. I allow the dough to rise and double in size in the refrigerator overnight. Once it has risen, it remains fresh for one day refrigerated. You can also freeze it for up to threee months. Defrost in the fridge overnight before working with it.

MAKES 9 ROLLS

- 1 recipe Mallorca dough (see page 193)
- 6 thick-cut bacon slices
- Flour, for dusting
- 1⅓ (packed) cups dark brown sugar
- 2 tablespoons plus ½ teaspoons ground cinnamon
- ¼ teaspoon ground cloves
- ½ teaspoon ground ginger
- 8 tablespoons (1 stick) salted butter, at room temperature, plus 8 tablespoons (1 stick) melted butter for brushing
- Oil, for greasing the baking sheets
- Confectioners' sugar, sifted, for serving

1. Make the Mallorca dough and let rise until doubled. It will take 1½ hours at room temp or 8 to 12 hours in the fridge.

2. Once the dough has risen, preheat oven to 400°F. Line a sheet pan with parchment, set a rack on top, and add the bacon in one layer. Bake 15 minutes or until crisp. Cool, then chop into ¼-inch pieces.

3. Flour your surface and roll dough into a rectangle slightly larger than 18 x 10 inches, about 1 inch thick.

4. In a medium bowl, mix brown sugar, cinnamon, cloves, ginger, and butter until smooth.

5. Spread filling evenly over dough. Cut into 9 strips (about 2 inches wide). Roll each into a tight spiral, tucking the end underneath.

6. Grease and line one large and one small rimmed sheet pan with parchment, also greasing the paper. Place rolls on top, at least 3 inches apart. Brush tops with 4 tablespoons melted butter and sprinkle with bacon. Cover loosely with plastic wrap and a towel. Let rise 30 minutes in a warm spot.

7. Preheat oven to 350°F with racks in upper and lower thirds. Remove covers. Brush rolls with the remaining melted butter. Bake 25 to 28 minutes, rotating pans top to bottom and front to back halfway through, until puffed and golden.

8. After 5 minutes, transfer to a wire rack to cool. Dust generously with confectioners' sugar and serve.

MALLORCAS

Rich, tender, and irresistibly sweet, mallorcas are a Puerto Rican culinary treasure. These classic eggy sweet rolls originated in Spain and boast a soft, airy texture and a delightfully buttery flavor. Enjoy these on their own, dusted with a mountain of powdered sugar, or as the base for my Pan de Mallorca Bacon Cinnamon Rolls (page 190).

This dough is made with quite a few egg yolks. Reserve all the egg whites for a different recipe. You can make this dough ahead and allow it to rise overnight in the fridge. Once it has risen it will remain fresh for one day in the refrigerator. You can also freeze it for up to three months. Defrost in the fridge overnight before working with it.

Once baked, you can freeze the buns (without garnishing with powdered sugar) for up to three months as well. Defrost in the fridge overnight and toast in a 350°F oven for a few minutes until warmed through. Finish with a heavy dusting of powdered sugar.

MAKES 12 ROLLS

- 2 cups warm milk (no more than 110°F)
- 2¼ teaspoons (¼ ounce) active dry or instant yeast
- 8 large egg yolks
- ⅓ cup granulated sugar
- 1 teaspoon kosher salt
- 20 tablespoons (2½ sticks) salted butter, melted and cooled, divided
- 6 cups bread flour, plus more for dusting
- ½ teaspoon oil, for greasing
- ¼ cup powdered sugar for garnish

NOTE: Opt for a light-colored sheet pan when it's time to bake. Dark sheet pans retain more heat than light ones and can burn the bottoms of your mallorcas.

1. In the bowl of a stand mixer (not yet on its stand), pour in the milk then sprinkle the yeast on the surface. Let that sit for 1 to 2 minutes. (If the yeast does not activate, pour out the milk and start over with new yeast.) Add the egg yolks, sugar, salt, and 16 tablespoons of the butter, mixing until well incorporated.

2. Using a whisk or flexible spatula, incorporate the flour into the mixture, adding it 2 cups at a time. Place the bowl on the stand mixer fitted with a dough-hook attachment and knead on low speed for several minutes, to form a sticky dough that partially pulls away from the sides of the bowl. Stop to scrape down the bowl.

3. Grease a large bowl with the oil and scrape the dough into it, turning the dough over to coat. Cover with a clean towel and set in a warm, draft-free spot to rise until doubled in size, about 1 hour 30 minutes.

4. Line two light-colored baking sheets with parchment paper.

5. Generously flour a clean work surface. Turn the dough out onto the surface and sprinkle with additional flour. Cut the dough into 12 equal pieces. Roll each dough piece into a ½-inch-thick rope.

6. To form the buns, place one end of one rope on the floured surface and begin winding it around itself to form a snail shell shape. Keep winding the rope until you reach the end. Then tuck the final end of the rope underneath the coiled bun to secure it.

7. Place 6 rolls on each prepared baking sheet. Loosely cover with a kitchen towel or plastic wrap and let rise for 45 minutes.

8. Preheat the oven to 350°F. Gently brush the tops of the rolls with the remaining 4 tablespoons of butter. Bake for 20-25 minutes, or until lightly golden brown.

9. Let the rolls cool completely before generously dusting with powdered sugar.

Meant to Be Guzzled

Cafés, Sodas, and Other Drinks

MAMEY LASSI

Mamey tastes like cantaloupe and sweet potatoes had a fling. This fruit's salmon-colored flesh is firm but succulent, earthy with honey notes. When the fruit on our kitchen counter was attracting more flies than hands, my grandmother added the mamey to her ancient Osterizer blender to make a *batida,* a sort of thick and chunky milkshake without the ice cream. She pulverized the fruit with a little evaporated milk and ice to keep us cool in the blistering summer heat. This Spanglish mashup uses a mix of Indian-inspired cardamom and yogurt to take mamey to a new level.

SERVES 2

1 cup frozen/defrosted mamey pulp (may substitute with peeled, chopped ripe mamey fruit)

2 cups very cold whole or low-fat milk

½ cup full-fat or low-fat Greek yogurt

2 tablespoons honey, plus more as needed

½ teaspoon ground cardamom

⅛ teaspoon ground ginger

Pinch of kosher salt, for serving

1. In a blender, puree the mamey and whole milk until smooth.

2. Add the yogurt, honey, cardamom, and ginger. Puree until fully incorporated and smooth. Taste, and add more honey as needed.

3. Divide the lassi between 2 large glasses. Season with the pinch of salt over each glass and serve.

VEGAN ACHIOTE LATTE

SERVES 1

½ cup coconut milk, well shaken

1 tablespoon annatto seeds

1 teaspoon ground ginger

Whole nutmeg

Pinch of kosher salt

1 teaspoon granulated sugar, plus more as needed

In Puerto Rico, the best coffee shops are often the ones that look a little tired around the edges. The paint's peeling, the vinyl floors are dull, and the ceiling fan wobbles just enough to make you hope you're not there when it finally decides to drop. You don't go there to be seen, as much as you go to commune.

In Los Angeles, coffee shops feel more like theaters, like everyone's auditioning for a role called themselves but more interesting. Nobody's shouting "¡Buenos días!" (Good morning!) across the room. They're too busy avoiding eye contact, typing quietly, "manifesting".

As strange as coffee shops in LA feel to me, I do love the ridiculous selection of caffeinated beverages, especially golden lattes made with turmeric and warming spices. This is my Puerto Rican take, made with achiote (annatto) instead of turmeric. It pairs perfectly with coconut milk.

1. In a small saucepan, over medium-high heat, whisk together the coconut milk, annatto seeds, ginger, a few gratings of nutmeg, the pinch of salt, and ½ cup water. Bring to a boil, at which point the mixture will pick up color from the annatto seeds, then remove from the heat and steep for 5 minutes.

2. Stir the mixture and return it to the stovetop over medium heat. Cook for 1 to 2 minutes, until the mixture just begins to steam.

3. Then using a fine-mesh strainer, strain directly into a heatproof cup, discarding the solids. Add the sugar, stirring until dissolved. Taste and add more sugar if needed. Serve hot.

SESAME SEED HORCHATA

On the island, there are street vendors on almost every major throughway, selling Chiclets and fresh fruit, and sometimes homemade sesame seed brittle known as *dulce de ajonjolí*. These roadside candies can be hard enough to chip a tooth, but they are irresistible once you get a taste of them. I make this horchata to recreate the flavors I grew up with and keep my teeth intact.

SERVES 4

- 1 cup toasted sesame seeds
- 2 (3-inch) Ceylon cinnamon sticks (soft/easily crumbled variety), broken into pieces
- 4 cups water
- 1½ cups dairy milk or almond milk
- ⅓ cup granulated sugar, plus more as needed
- 2 teaspoons vanilla extract
- 2 teaspoons ground cinnamon
- Ice, for serving (optional)

NOTE: Ceylon cinnamon is crumbly and breakable, and has a distinct aroma. A Latino pantry item, it's sold in bags at Latino markets.

1. In a blender, combine the sesame seeds, cinnamon sticks, and 2 cups of the water. Puree for about 2 minutes, or until the sesame seeds and cinnamon sticks are coarsely ground. Add the remaining 2 cups of water and blend again until uniform in color (tan), with only small bits of visible cinnamon.

2. Transfer the mixture into an airtight container, seal, and let it sit at room temperature for 8 hours, to develop the flavors. Give it a swirl when it looks like it has separated.

3. Set a fine-mesh strainer over a pitcher. Pour/scrape the rested mixture through, extracting as much liquid as possible. Discard the solids.

4. In a small saucepan, over medium-low heat, warm through 1 cup of the dairy milk. Stir in the sugar until completely dissolved. Then add the remaining ½ cup of dairy milk, the vanilla, and ground cinnamon. Taste, and add more sugar if needed.

5. Mix the sweetened milk mixture into the strained sesame seed horchata. Seal the pitcher and refrigerate for at least 1 hour, or until well chilled. Mix well before serving. Serve as is, or over ice, if using.

MALTA FLOAT

My mother loved to mix malta, the fizzy nonalcoholic malt beverage, with milk and chug it as she chain smoked and talked *bochinche* (gossip), with her sisters. It's an absolute knockout when layered with ice cream and condensed milk. A touch of chocolate sauce takes things over the top.

SERVES 1

- 1 tablespoon chocolate syrup (try my recipe for Annatto, Coconut, and Dark Chocolate Syrup, page 162, or store-bought)
- 3 tablespoons sweetened condensed milk
- 12 ounces chilled malta
- 1 scoop vanilla ice cream (about ½ cup)

1. In a large glass, drizzle in the chocolate syrup in one layer.
2. Top it with the sweetened condensed milk in a second layer.
3. Gently pour in the malta.
4. Top with the ice cream and serve.

SOURSOP FIZZ

Soursop is like the Beast from *Beauty and the Beast*. It's monstrously ugly on the outside yet magically delicate on the inside. I give it a glow-up by taking its milky flesh and making it a base for a citrusy fizz. You can transform this into a grown-up cocktail with a touch of white rum, to taste.

SERVES 4

- 1 tablespoon well-shaken cream of coconut
- ½ teaspoon peeled, finely grated fresh ginger root
- ¼ cup frozen/defrosted soursop puree or pulp
- 2 teaspoons fresh lime juice
- 4 cups plain club soda or seltzer water
- Simple syrup (see Tip)
- Ice cubes, for serving

1. In a large pitcher, stir together the cream of coconut and the ginger. Let that sit for 5 minutes, then add the soursop puree, lime juice, and club soda. Mix well.

2. Taste and adjust to your preferred sweetness with simple syrup. Add the ice, stir until well chilled, and serve.

TIP: To make simple syrup combine equal parts sugar and water in a saucepan over medium heat, stirring until the sugar dissolves. Remove from heat and let it cool. Store in an airtight container in the refrigerator for up to 2 months.

TAMARIND SWEET TEA

The farm I grew up on in Boquerón had a huge tamarind tree at its entrance. On our way to run errands in the city, my abuelo made it a habit to stop at the tree and gather the brittle pods for my brother and me to feast on. We sat wide-eyed in the back seat of his beat-up baby blue Fiat, our mouths watering with expectation. Tamarind was our favorite candy.

If you've never had fresh tamarind, the brown shell cracks open to reveal sticky brown flesh wrapped around large black seeds. The fruit is deeply flavored and very tart, as if Mother Nature tasted sour gummies and then said, "Hold my beer."

Please note that tamarind pulp comes in multiple forms. You can find it frozen in a juicy puree form, which I prefer to use in drinks. You'll also find it at room temperature in block form, which needs to be hydrated with hot water and then pressed through a sieve to remove any fibers. This will have the brightest and most intense tamarind flavor. You can also find it in a "paste puree," a thick, brown-textured paste with duller flavor; or "paste concentrate," a viscous, smooth, almost black gel with a very tart flavor. Sometimes these pastes may also be salted. They're best used for savory sauces like my Tamarind Guava BBQ Sauce (page 52). For convenience, I've used frozen tamarind pulp in this recipe. But if you have the time, rehydrate and strain a cup of tamarind block and use that. It's divine!

To make a Passion Fruit and Tamarind Arnold Palmer, combine this with Passion Fruit Lemonade (page 206).

SERVES 4
(MAKES ABOUT
7 CUPS)

¾ cup of simple syrup, or more to taste (see Tip)

6 cups water

3 black-tea bags (good quality tea)

14 ounces frozen tamarind pulp

1 lime, cut into thin rounds (wheels), plus more for garnish

Ice

TIP: To make simple syrup, combine equal parts sugar and water in a saucepan over medium heat, stirring until the sugar dissolves. Remove from heat and let it cool. Store in an airtight container in the refrigerator for up to 2 months.

1. In a medium saucepan, over medium-high heat, bring the water to a boil, then remove from the heat. Add the tea bags and steep for about 5 minutes, or until dark and fragrant. Discard the tea bags.

2. Pour the tea mixture into a gallon-size pitcher and add the simple syrup. Add the frozen tamarind pulp to help cool the tea. Stir until defrosted and well blended. Taste and add more simple syrup as needed. Add the lime wheels to the tea.

3. Just before serving, add enough ice to fill the pitcher. Serve once the tamarind tea is well chilled.

PASSION FRUIT LEMONADE

Passion fruit juice is an everyday joy in Puerto Rico, where the vines grow wild and people are trying to use up as much of the fruit as they can. I add it to lemon juice for a truly tart spin on lemonade. The real flex is combining it with Tamarind Sweet Tea (page 205) to make a Passion Fruit and Tamarind Arnold Palmer.

SERVES 4 (MAKES ABOUT 6 CUPS)

½ cup fresh lemon juice (from 3 to 4 large lemons)

14 ounces frozen/defrosted passion fruit pulp

4 cups cold water, plus more as needed

¾ cup Simple Syrup (see Tip), plus more as needed

Lemon rounds, for garnish

1. In a large pitcher, combine the lemon juice and passion fruit pulp. Add the cold water and simple syrup, stirring to mix well.
2. Taste, and if needed, add more water and/or simple syrup to achieve the perfect balance of sweet and tart.
3. Cover and refrigerate until well chilled. Stir again just before serving. Garnish with lemon rounds.

TIP: To make simple syrup, combine equal parts sugar and water in a saucepan over medium heat, stirring until the sugar dissolves. Remove from heat and let it cool. Store in an airtight container in the refrigerator for up to 2 months.

CAFÉ COLAO MILKSHAKE

One of my earliest memories is of sitting in my Abuela Alicia's tiny apartment in San Juan. I was five years old and the roar of the highway just outside her window was a sort of soundtrack to her morning routine. The cars honked angrily as she prepared her *café colao* the same way she had ten thousand times before. She would make me a cup, more milk and sugar than coffee, and I would gulp it down as I listened to her gossip on the phone with my *tías*.

This Café Colao Milkshake brings me back to those early mornings with my abuela, and it never fails to stamp a huge grin on my face. I hope it does the same for you.

SERVES 2

- 1¼ cups freshly brewed espresso or strong pour-over, cooled
- ⅛ teaspoon ground cinnamon, plus more for garnish
- Pinch of ground star anise
- Pinch of kosher salt
- ¼ cup sweetened condensed milk
- 1 cup whole milk
- 2 cups coffee-flavored ice cream
- Whipped cream, for garnish

1. In a blender, combine the espresso, cinnamon, the pinch of star anise, the pinch of salt, and the sweetened condensed milk. Puree for about 20 seconds, or until velvety.
2. Add the whole milk and ice cream. Puree until smooth and thick.
3. Divide the milkshake between 2 glasses. Top each with whipped cream, dust with cinnamon, and serve.

Conclusion

Never Mind the Food Police

I once had a Puerto Rican chef tell me that I have a responsibility to represent "our" food "authentically." They whispered it in the gravest of tones as they took a long drag of a Parliament Light. "You cannot call your beans Puerto Rican if you make them with olives," they exhaled hurriedly in a cloud of smoke, as if explaining the rules of the world to a child. "It's not the way it's done," they finished, "even if that's how your abuela did it."

I was rankled.

To keep me quiet as I watched her make red beans, my Abuela Dora would sneak me olives. I loved the way the green ringlets floated to the top of the broth like polka dots, the way she would snag them with a fork like a professional olive harpooner, and, most of all, the pop of acidity that washed over my tongue when I bit them gently. I don't make red beans without olives; it erases my abuela from a recipe that shaped me. Does that make me less Puerto Rican?

Food speaks, with refreshing honesty, of culture, history, and perhaps most importantly, of personal story. It's not a museum exhibit locked behind glass. It's a universal language. And like any language, it evolves. Just because we no longer speak the native tongue of our island's first inhabitants, doesn't mean their blood doesn't run through our veins. Adapting doesn't erase our identity; it reflects our resilience.

Maybe that's why I find the Puerto Rican "food police" so baffling. They're the self-appointed neighborhood watch of food, armed with rigid notions of "authenticity" and loud pronouncements of, "*Así no se hace*." ("That's not how it's done.") They patrol the borders of culinary expression, attempting to control what constitutes a dish's "true" representation, as if there's only one right way. As if our food hasn't always been shaped by migration, colonization, hunger, and invention.

Don't get me wrong. Preserving our heritage matters. But insisting that Puerto Ricans adhere to culinary tradition or relinquish their identity creates a cuisine frozen in amber, one that is as brittle as the coconut candy my abuelo was so fond of. Must Puerto Rican food always mirror that of the *jíbaros*, our country farmers, to be considered genuine?

And what makes the cuisine of the jíbaro more authentic than that of the Taíno? Puerto Rico's Indigenous people ate seafood, root vegetables, and native plants. It was Spanish colonizers and enslaved Africans who brought many of the ingredients we now consider traditional: pork, rice, cod, plantains, coffee, spices. It was the enslaved African women, using whatever scraps they could get their hands on along with techniques brought from their motherland, who created many of the dishes that became the foundation of *la cocina criolla,* Puerto Rico's traditional cuisine.

If we celebrate the changes the Spanish and the Africans brought, why do we reject the effects of American colonization and the migration that followed? Maybe it's because the relationship between Puerto Rico and the United States has always been complicated–and more often than not, painful.

The United States invaded Puerto Rico in 1898, and has been using it for its own gain ever since. Puerto Ricans were handed US citizenship–not as a gift, but as a tool of control. It's citizenship without power. Islanders can fight in US wars, but can't vote for a president, don't have electoral representation, and have no full voice in Congress, even though they outnumber the populations of twenty US states.

Not long ago, waving the Puerto Rican flag could get you jailed. Advocating for independence made you a "terrorist." The US government even forcibly sterilized Puerto Rican women to control the population on the island. And though those tactics have changed, the choke hold on the people of Borikén hasn't gone anywhere. It just looks different now.

Boricuas live with unfair tax laws that help big US companies and ultra-rich Continental Americans, but hurt Puerto Rican people. Take the Jones Act, for example, which states any goods shipped by boat between US ports must be carried on ships that are built in the United States, owned by Americans, and crewed by Americans. With no competition from other countries, prices for everyday goods and produce can soar to nearly double what you'd pay in the Lower 48, while the quality often hits rock bottom. This is a death blow on an island that imports 85 percent of its food.

Puerto Ricans also live under *La Junta*, a fiscal oversight board no one on the island elected, put in place by the US government to help restructure billions of dollars in debt. But instead of helping Puerto Rican people, 40 percent of which live beneath the poverty line, the board has prioritized Wall Street. It's forcing islanders to pay back a debt that wasn't created by them but by decades of government corruption, fiscal mismanagement, and colonial policy. It isn't the politicians or the investors who are paying the price. It's teachers, retirees, students, and families who've had their pensions slashed, schools closed, and healthcare gutted.

The list of injustices goes on and on. The citizens of Puerto Rico suffer hundreds of blackouts a year under LUMA, a private energy company owned by the United States and Canada that charges the highest rates in America for third-world reliability. Puerto Ricans are being priced out of their own neighborhoods by Act 60, a law that gives massive tax breaks to wealthy people from the continental US who move to the island to play in paradise. Even though beach access is supposed to be protected by law, new developments backed by US investors are cutting off public access or using armed security guards to force Puerto Ricans off the very beaches they grew up on. These are just some of the reasons more Puerto Ricans now live stateside than on the island itself.

And if this continues—if the land keeps getting sold off, if the lights stay out more than they stay on, if the cost of living keeps soaring while the island's voices get smaller—we're staring down something unthinkable: a Puerto Rico without Puerto Ricans. An island stripped for parts and sold to the highest bidder. And the people who built it, fed it, raised generations on it? Pushed out. Priced out. Forgotten. Not by accident, but by design.

So it's no wonder why so many Puerto Ricans bristle at the idea of their food being "Americanized." When the same government that's stripped your island of power, both literally and politically, wants to lay claim to your culinary identity, it hits different. Food is one of the few things we still have that feels *ours*. It's not just tradition. It's resistance. To dilute it, rename it, or repackage it for the "mainland" palate can feel like one more kind of erasure, one more way to be told who we are by people who've never had to hold on tight to identity to keep it from slipping away.

But if we demand that our cuisine stay frozen in time, we erase the very creativity and resilience that built it. *La Cocina Criolla* was born out of blending, adapting, and reimagining. We honor our ancestors not by cooking exactly as they did, but by carrying their spirit forward. Holding on to tradition should never mean holding back progress.

It also means accepting the lived experiences of millions of Puerto Ricans who grew up in the Bronx, Orlando, Philly, or Chicago—people who can't find culantro at the supermarket, so they use store-bought sofrito. *Puertorros* who eat pasteles wrapped in foil instead of banana leaves and smother them in ketchup instead of pique because they make do with what they have. These stateside Boricuas keep the spirit of *La Cocina Criolla* alive in the diaspora, in school cafeterias, in corner bodegas, and in cramped apartment kitchens. And though it might look a little different, *that's* Puerto Rican, too.

Our food tells our story. And our story is complicated. Accepting change doesn't erase our roots. It proves they're still growing. The real danger isn't change. The real danger is believing there's only one way to be Boricua, only one way to cook Puerto Rican food.

Puerto Rico is one of the oldest colonies in the world. It has endured over a century of economic extraction, a crippling wave of migration, and exile from true political power—and still it stands. But if we want our cuisine to do more than just exist, if we want it to thrive, it can't be shackled the same way the island has been. Tradition matters, yes. But so does truth. Puerto Rican food has never been untouched. It has never been pure. It has always been shaped by struggle, survival, and spirit.

Colonization has changed La Cocina Criolla forever. There is no going back.

Pa'lante. (Forward.)

If you're Spanglish, like me, your Puerto Rican-ness is always up for debate, by those on the big continent and those on the island.

"¡Pero dímelo en español!" ("Tell me in Spanish.")

"You don't look Puerto Rican."

"¿No bailas salsa?" ("You don't dance salsa?")

"You're not really Puerto Rican if you didn't grow up there, right?"

"Puertorriqueños de verdad no hacen sofrito así." ("Real Puerto Ricans don't make sofrito like that.")

"You're Puerto Rican? Where's your flag?"

These moments sting like mosquitoes, unexpected and sharp. You swat them away, but they itch for days. They make you question. They make you shrink. They whisper: *You're not enough.*

But here's the truth: no one—*nadie*—gets to strip you of your identity because you're made different than the original model. Being Puerto Rican isn't about how well you speak English or Spanish. It isn't about the color of your skin or how well you can move your feet. And it sure as hell isn't about how you make your sofrito.

Being Puerto Rican is in your blood. It's something no one can take away from you. It's the pride that engulfs you when you see our flag dangling from a rearview mirror, even if you don't have one on yours. It's what makes you scream, *"Boricua!"* when you meet someone with ties to the island, transforming strangers into instant family. It's what brings a lump to your throat when you hear "En Mi Viejo San Juan." ("In My Old San Juan.") That's real. That's what matters. That's what makes you Boricua.

So, yes, I'm pale and I pass, but that doesn't mean I'm "white." I can't dance salsa, but the rhythmic rasp of a guiro hooks me every time. I've lived more years on the big continent than I've lived on the island, but as soon as I hear a coquí sing, I'm home.

You're going to need to slow it down when you speak to me in Spanish, and I'm going to answer you in Spanglish. I make my sofrito with bell peppers, my rice with butter, and my red beans with olives. They're delicious and they're Puerto Rican.

Just. Like. Me.

Like my Abuela Dora would say, *"No jodas. Hay mucho que hacer."* ("Don't fuss around. There's work to be done.")

Acknowledgments

This book would not exist without the love, generosity, and guidance of so many people who shaped me, both in and out of the kitchen.

To my Abuela Dora, who taught me my very first recipes with patience and love, and to my Abuelo Quique, who quietly instilled in me a lifelong devotion to all things pastry. Thank you for lighting the spark that defined me.

To my Abuela Alicia, who taught me to love coffee and the stories that come with it. Thank you for showing me that the most important things in life are often shared across a table, one sip at a time.

To my mother, Myriam—whose towering cookbook collection and hours spent in the kitchen used to puzzle me. I see it now. Thank you for teaching me before I even knew I was learning.

To my father, Ricardo—though you weren't around for most of my life, thank you for the impact you had, even from afar. I hope one day we get the chance to truly know each other.

To my siblings Joel, Marji, Kian, Rich, Joey, Diego, and Richie—thank you for being there when life felt heavy. Our bond hasn't always followed a straight path, but in the moments that mattered most, each of you showed up in your own way. I'll always carry that with me.

To my son, Danger—my greatest love. There were too many days when I didn't know how we were going to make it, but you gave me something worth fighting for. This book exists because I refused to give up, and I refused to give up because of you.

To my all-time favorite teacher, Susan Hunt—thank you for changing my life. Your classroom was where writing stopped being an assignment and started feeling like home.

To Ken Park—my brother Joel's lifelong best friend, and my unexpected lifeline. You moved in during one of the darkest chapters of my life and asked for nothing but home-cooked meals. Thank you for giving me the courage to begin again.

To Dianne Jacob—thank you for believing in my voice before I fully believed in it myself. You shaped my book proposal with such care, edited my earliest food essays with clarity and heart, and showed me that my stories were worth telling.

To my literary agent, Sally Ekus, who took a Zoom call with a stranger in the height of the pandemic and somehow spun it into a book deal with Simon & Schuster. Thank you for the countless hours, for always picking up the phone, and for walking beside me every step of the way.

To Doris Cooper, my editor. I was 150 miles away from polished during our first meeting, and still, you said yes. That yes changed my life. Thank you for seeing the soul in this book before a single recipe had been written and for trusting me to tell this story my way.

To Veronica Alvarado—thank you for reviewing this manuscript with such care and respect. You challenged me to dig deeper, say it clearer, and stand taller in my voice.

To Bonnie Benwick, who tested every recipe with a precision and thoughtfulness that lifted this book from good to great. You caught what

I missed, challenged what needed refining, and honored the heart of every dish.

To those of you who subscribed to *Spanglish* back when it was just a handful of hopeful posts on Substack—thank you. Veronica Ocasio, Rocco DiSpirito, Charlene Badman, JR Schuman, Gwen Trotter, Jason Kelso, Kevin Eddington, Olivier Amar, Brooke Streicher, Erin Carman, Caesar Alfano, Bex Streeper—you were there at the beginning, and I'll never forget it.

To Rafael N. Ruiz Mederos, Keila Rivera, Eilane Batista, Leilany Herrera, and Carlos Marrero Landrón—thank you for helping me bring this book to life on a minimal budget with maximum heart. What we lacked in experience, we made up for with pure love for our island and a deep desire to help pave the road for other Puerto Rican creatives in the food space. You stepped up to every challenge with grace and together we made magic. Thank you for believing in this project, and for giving it your all. #NoBarriers

To Giovanna Huyke—thank you for deepening my understanding of our food, its history, and its soul. You've been an inspiration, not just to me, but to our island and the diaspora. I am honored to call you my friend.

To the chefs of Puerto Rico—every day, you face challenges that would make most people quit: unreliable power, limited resources, economic instability, political neglect. And still, you show up. You cook with brilliance, tell stories through food, and turn struggle into artistry. You inspire me to be a better person. To do more. To push harder. You are my constant reminder that greatness often comes not from ease, but from resilience.

To my beautiful island of Puerto Rico and the friends and family that live there—you are my whole heart. You guided me, raised me, and fed me in every way that matters. Your spirit, your struggle, and your joy live on every page of this book. You are the reason I tell stories, and the reason I believe food can be a form of healing and of homecoming.

To Andrew Zimmern—thank you for picking up the phone when things got hard and for reminding me to focus on the present. Your guidance and belief in me kept me going when I didn't think I could.

To Gordon Ramsay—thank you for giving me an apron when I auditioned for *MasterChef*. I had no idea that tying those strings around my waist would mark the start of a new life. But it did. Everything changed the moment you believed I was ready for that kitchen, because all of a sudden, I believed it, too.

And finally, to you, dear reader. Maybe you know exactly what it feels like to grow up in the in-between, never fully one thing, never fully the other. Maybe you're Puerto Rican, and you feel this book in your bones. Maybe you're someone trying to understand, or someone who's followed my journey for years, post by post, plate by plate. Thank you for being here and for reading to the very end.

My deepest hope is that these stories and recipes either help you feel seen or help you see better. I hope *Spanglish* teaches you, like it did me, that identity isn't something you have to choose, it's something you get to create. It is your greatest recipe.

xoxo—Monti

Index

NOTE: Page references in *italics* refer to photos.

D

E

F

G

H

I

J

L

M

N

O

P

Q

R

S

T

V

A delicious tribute to Puerto Rican cuisine and culture, with more than sixty-five soulful recipes

Growing up, Monti Carlo felt like she was perpetually bridging the gap between worlds—one foot on her home island of Puerto Rico, and the other in the heart of Houston, Texas. In the space between, as a self-taught chef and eventual TV host and James Beard Foundation advisor, she's carved out a cuisine all her own, one that's a testament to a life spent bridging two cultures. It's a mosaic of borrowed words and flavors, a reflection of the bittersweet beauty of connecting two very different ways of life. It's pure *Spanglish*.

Within these pages, Monti shares the dishes embodying that journey: continental American classics created with the bold flavors of Puerto Rico, a taste of two worlds merging on the same plate. There's comfort food like her elementary school's soupy chili with her Abuela Dora's sweet and savory picadillo, golden bacalaíto-battered onion rings, and tangy tamarind roast chicken. There are nostalgia-laced Puerto Rican breakfasts like hearty sorullo waffles with pique honey and pastries like cinnamon rolls constructed with pillowy mallorca dough. There are not-so-traditional sides like floral hibiscus baked beans and crispy coconut rice. And there's delectable, subtly sweet desserts like *morir soñando* no-bake cheesecake and passion fruit-curd stuffed mini cakes. There's also a glossary of traditional Puerto Rican ingredients and where to source them, as well as recipes for traditional Puerto Rican bases like sofrito, sazón, and recaito.

With flavor and heart, this cookbook is more than just recipes. It's a beautifully written reflection on Boricua identity and a testament to the healing power of food.